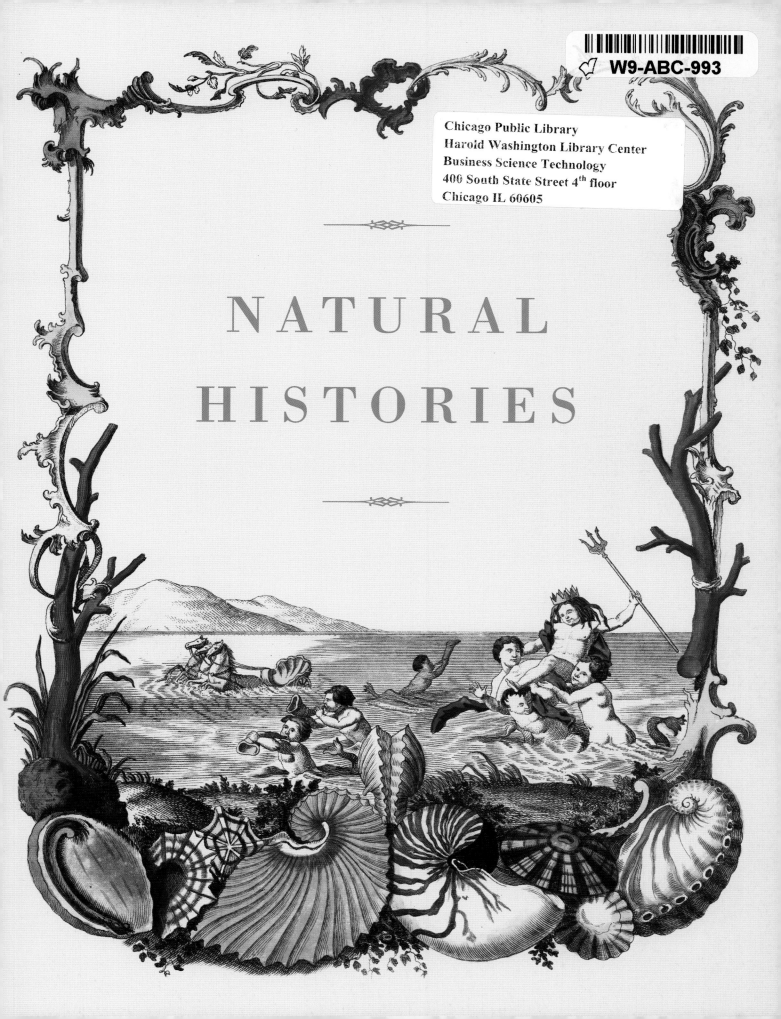

NATURAL HISTORIES

Sterling Signature
NEW YORK

An Imprint of Sterling Publishing
387 Park Avenue South
New York, NY 10016

ISBN 978-1-4027-9149-9

Library of Congress Cataloging-in-Publication Data

Natural histories : extraordinary selections from the rare book archive of
  the American Museum of Natural History Library / edited by Tom Baione.
    p. cm.
  ISBN 978-1-4027-9149-9
  1. Natural history—Bibliography—Catalogs. 2. Illustrated
books—Bibliography—Catalogs. 3. Rare books—Bibliography—Catalogs.
4. American Museum of Natural History. Library—Catalogs. I. Baione,
Tom.
  Z7409.N273 2012
  [QH45]
  016.508—dc23
                                    2012008399

Distributed in Canada by Sterling Publishing
c/o Canadian Manda Group, 165 Dufferin Street
Toronto, Ontario, Canada M6K 3H6
Distributed in the United Kingdom by GMC Distribution Services
Castle Place, 166 High Street, Lewes, East Sussex, England BN7 1XU
Distributed in Australia by Capricorn Link (Australia) Pty. Ltd.
P.O. Box 704, Windsor, NSW 2756, Australia

Cover and book design by Chin-Yee Lai

For information about custom editions, special sales,
and premium and corporate purchases, please contact Sterling Special Sales
at 800-805-5489 or specialsales@sterlingpublishing.com.

Manufactured in China

2 4 6 8 10 9 7 5 3

www.sterlingpublishing.com

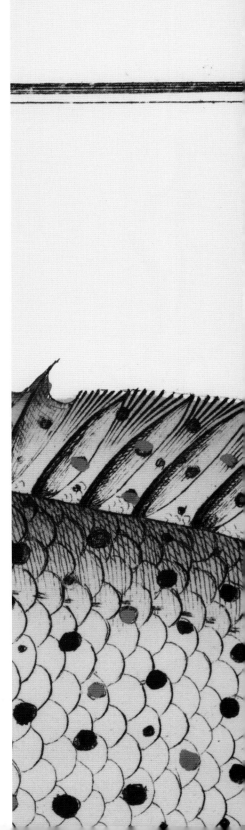

NATURAL HISTORIES

Extraordinary Rare Book Selections from

the American Museum of Natural History Library

Edited by

TOM BAIONE

Sterling Signature
NEW YORK

CONTENTS

Foreword

ELLEN V. FUTTER
President of the American Museum of Natural History

Since 1877, the Research Library of the American Museum of Natural History has been an indispensable resource for museum scientists and staff, researchers from around the world, and the general public. Today, housing more than half a million volumes, over 22,000 journal titles, and numerous special collections of photography, moving images, manuscripts, archives, art, and memorabilia, it embraces the history and current state of natural history and is one of the world's greatest natural history libraries. Since 1993, the library has been housed within the museum's Manhattan campus in a purpose-built, eight-story facility with nearly sixteen linear miles of shelving, state-of-the-art security, compact shelving, and four different climate zones for different kinds of materials.

But, as this book offers glorious testament, the Research Library is far more than statistics and facts. *Natural Histories* gathers some of the most scientifically significant, historically rare, and beautifully illustrated gems of the library's Rare Book Collections.

The museum—and one could argue the discipline of natural history itself—can be viewed as a lively and ever-changing conversation between the past and the present. And so this book has paired museum scientists and librarians with key historical works from the collection to create an intriguing dialogue of discovery. In doing so, it illuminates the beauty and wonder of the natural world and celebrates the intrinsically human impulse—transcending time and place—to explore and better understand the world around us, an impulse which is at the very heart of the museum's mission.

The first section of the museum complex was completed in 1877, and for some time stood alone in Manhattan Square, the early name for the museum's site. This view, looking southwest, shows the Vaux and Mould–designed structure amid a pond and rock outcrops, revealing the uneven nature of the terrain.

Introduction

TOM BAIONE

*Harold Boeschenstein Director of Library Services in the
Research Library at the American Museum of Natural History*

Within the walls of the American Museum of Natural History in New York City lies a collection of important rare book treasures. The museum's Research Library has been at the core of the museum since its founding in 1869. In fact, the first books became part of the museum's library while the newly chartered institution was still housed in temporary quarters at the Central Park Arsenal. In 1877, when the museum moved to its Upper West Side home, the museum's library had acquired a substantial book collection, which was then "moved into sky-lit rooms, complete with glass floors, and fitted with special cases and iron shelves" according to the unpublished biography of the museum's founder, Albert Bickmore.

The Research Library's mission was—and remains—to serve as a research tool for the American Museum of Natural History's staff to promote and produce science, exhibitions, and to help the education staff provide for public instruction, as the credo on our early bookplate states, "For the People, for Education, for Science." Any researcher is welcome to peruse a volume in the library's reading room, and museum staff are welcome to take old tomes to their offices for consultation. The Research Library continues to build its Rare Book Collections by adding discoveries from the library's general collection and from gifts and the occasional purchase.

Although many volumes now considered "rare" do bear the mark of having been sequestered from the library's general collection (the word "Safe" is written inside their front cover or on their title page), the museum's Research Library didn't always have a Rare Book Room or a Rare Book Collection. As the library's collection of rare books grew, it was moved several times before the first proper Rare Book Room was created in 1973. The collection then moved to its current, purpose-built storage facility in 1993, where the books are preserved and monitored under strict environmental conditions by a professional conservator, and where entry is subject to multilayered security procedures. A book is deemed "rare" for many reasons, such as scarcity, uniqueness, age, binding type, size, value, or illustrations—some so beguiling that people have been known to want to tear them out. More often then not, a rare book possesses a combination of several of these factors.

The prints in these books are, by definition, copies: they are not original art but reproductions of the originals. This is not to say that these prints are any less valuable scientifically. Indeed, in many significant ways they are more important than the originals. While the actual sketches or drawings might be thought to be closer to their subjects than the derived prints, these artworks are unique, final, and have limited exposure. The printmaking process allows for correction and clarification of the original art that is then printed and widely distributed. Prints are more important than the original art, as they are the emissaries responsible for spreading the "word"

A 1937 view of the Research Library's stacks. Notice the cast-iron shelves and floors, paved with glass block, that were originally set beneath skylights. Of course, now we know sunlight works against preservation efforts.

(and picture) far further than a single, original work ever could. In reaching a broader audience, the printed images consistently tell the same story, much like the printed text accompanying them.

Some prints included in this book may be familiar to some, others less so. How widely known the images are depends upon a number of factors, such as the size of the edition of the published work, who the artist was, and if the image was attractive or not. The makers of the books you will read about in this volume used a variety of increasingly sophisticated processes to create their printed illustrations. As technology progressed, so did the methods for producing even greater multitudes of identical images.

To fully appreciate the illustrations highlighted on the following pages, a short history of the various printing processes will help in understanding each image's origins. The earliest and simplest method for printing pictures was the relief method, in the form of woodcuts, which, as the name suggests, were carved into wooden blocks. Much like the later, moveable type surfaces that revolutionized printing in the late fifteenth century, woodcut prints were created by inking a reversed image and stamping it onto paper. Unfortunately, wood blocks were susceptible to cracking and breaking, and sharply carved wooden edges wore down after repeated use, producing increasingly duller results. Later the "intaglio" process, with its ability to create fine lines and thousands of identical impressions, rose to prominence.

The intaglio process (intaglio meaning "carving" in Italian) was very different from relief printing. Smooth sheets of copper were engraved, or carved, with lines and textures which were filled with ink. When the smooth surface of the sheet, or plate, was cleaned, paper was then pressed to the copper and pressure applied, allowing the paper to draw the ink out of the engraved lines. Later, portions of engraved images were exposed to acid in varying degrees to create softer lines and patterns, a process known as etching. Any of these black-and-white images could later be hand painted to render more realistic figures.

The great revolution in the printing of illustrations was lithography. Since copper was an expensive material—and talented engravers were few and far between—lithography, or printing from stone, became popular in the nineteenth century and led to an explosive increase in the number of illustrated works. In this method, an image is transferred directly to a stone printing surface by drawing or painting the image using specially formulated greasy inks in liquid or pencil form. The entire stone surface is then dampened and inked with a roller. Ink is repelled by wet stone, and the ink sticks only to the greasy image. Paper and pressure are applied to the stone's surface and the image is transferred to the paper.

The goal of many works on natural history has been to illustrate the scientific topic at hand, but from the infancy of printing, great artists were called on to further illuminate scientific text. In the earliest days of natural history illustration, artists had very limited information about the subjects at best, leading to inaccurate depictions. In many cases, the authors themselves were talented artists and created accurate illustrations to accompany their own texts. Some authors even trained as artists or honed their printmaking skills to enable them to illustrate and print the images they wished to reproduce as realistically as possible. Sometimes this led to art that depicted its intended subject accurately; sometimes it did not—as many times neither the author nor the artist had ever seen the subject or visited the place depicted. Often, the best

An early bookplate from the museum's library.

The rare folios are allowed to lie flat in an effort to protect their binding structure and contents. John Gould's *The mammals of Australia* is in the foreground.

illustrations resulted from partnerships between illustrators and the scientists who contracted them for the added value their artistic expertise lent to the written descriptions. Sadly, the identities of many of the artists cooperating with authors featured in this book have been lost to history.

It was very difficult to choose which items to highlight in this book from such a large and varied collection, so we limited our search to only those items with unusual or interesting illustrations—ones that spark curiosity in the viewer and a desire to learn more about their origins. Many of the more popular and familiar works were passed over in the selection in favor of those whose stories are seldom shared but are worth hearing, and whose illustrations, while not always beautiful in a conventional fashion, deserve notice from a scientific perspective and from an aesthetic one as well. Finally, authors were found among the ranks of the museum's scientists, associates, and librarians, whose work and interests had some affinity with the highlighted materials. These members of the museum community were then invited to write essays about each work, its author, its unique and rare components, and its contribution to and place in the history of natural science.

The books included range from the earliest printed sixteenth-century zoologies meant to reveal how animals looked, to twentieth-century works, where natural forms are celebrated for both their forms and beauty. The subjects covered reflect the disciplines studied at the American Museum of Natural History, including anthropology, paleontology, earth science, astronomy, and zoology, and range across all seven continents. Many themes are repeated throughout the stories of the creation of the books: family members and colleagues pitching in to help fund publishing projects or complete the writing; printed illustrations surviving as the only documentation of an organism's existence; and young travelers, scientists, and amateur science-lovers so fascinated by places, peoples, and creatures that they devoted their lives to documenting them and unraveling their mysteries. The stories behind the works selected, these *natural histories*, not only tell the story of the history of science and art over the last five hundred years, but also of the advances and revelations of science and technology during the age of print. While still tools for science, these works endure as small monuments to the achievements and struggles involved in the study of natural science over the centuries.

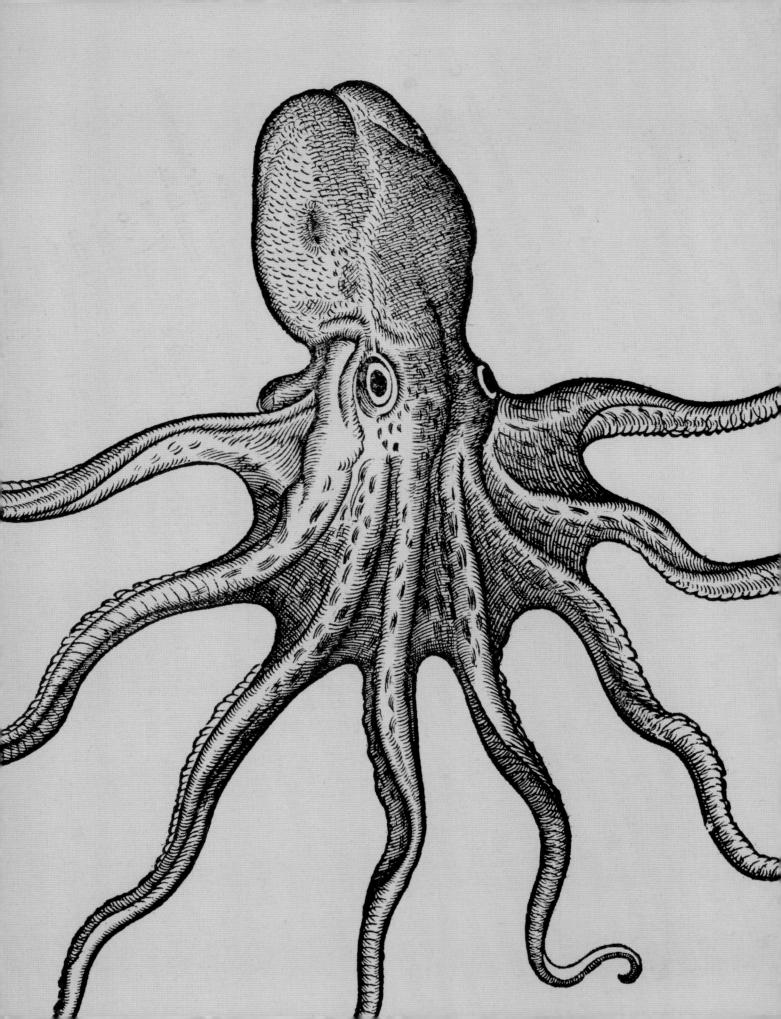

The First Animal Book

RICHARD ELLIS

Author
Conrad Gessner
(1516–1565)

Title
Historia animalium

(Histories of the animals)

Imprint
Tiguri: Apud Christoph.
Froschoverum,
1551–1558

Conrad Gessner (a.k.a. Konrad Gesner, Conradus Gessnerus, etc.) was born in Zurich on March 26, 1516, and died there on December 13, 1565. His five-volume *Historia animalium* (*Histories of the animals*) was published between 1551 and 1558, and is considered the beginning of modern zoology. The first volume is an illustrated work on live-bearing four-footed animals (mammals). Volume 2 is on egg-laying quadrupeds (crocodiles and lizards)—Australia's platypus and echidna hadn't been discovered yet. Volume 3 is on birds, and Volume 4 is on fish and other aquatic animals. A fifth volume on serpents (snakes and scorpions) was published posthumously in 1587. The *Historia animalium* was Gessner's magnum opus, and was the most widely read of all the Renaissance natural histories. The work was so popular that his own abridgement, *Thierbuch* (*Animal book*), was published in Zurich in 1563, complete with hand-colored woodcut illustrations.

The *Historia animalium* is an attempt to fashion a connection between the ancient knowledge of the animal world and Renaissance science. Gessner's monumental work is based on the Old Testament, Hebrew, Greek, and Latin sources, and is compiled from folklore as well as ancient and medieval texts, as many of the animals' names appear in Greek and Hebrew. For living animals, he incorporated the inherited knowledge of ancient naturalists like Aristotle, Pliny, and Aelian, and for information on mythical animals—which he usually identified as such—he drew from folktales, myths, and legends, some of which came from material in the *Physiologus*, a book of animal legends that was produced in Alexandria in the second century and subsequently translated into Syrian, Arabic, Armenian, Ethiopian, Latin, German, French, Provençal, Icelandic, Italian, and Anglo-Saxon. The *Physiologus* was not a single work in serial translations, but rather an ongoing work in progress with no single author and with material added and modified as the work wandered through time and geography. The *Physiologus* was translated into Latin in the eighth century and eventually evolved into a medieval bestiary and then into the *Historia animalium*.

Though Gessner sought to distinguish facts from folklore, his encyclopedic work also includes mythical creatures and imaginary beasts, mingled with unknown animals from the New World, the Far North (the publication coincided with the early searches for the Northeast and Northwest Passages), and newly discovered animals of the Indies. (Dürer's famous rhinoceros, originally drawn in 1515, appears in Volume 1 of the *Historia*.) Where appropriate, Gessner documented the uses of animals and animal products in medicine and nutrition, alongside their places in history, literature, and art.

1. Correct in most of its particulars, Gessner's octopus has the wrong eyes. Until people saw living octopuses (the correct plural), nobody knew that their pupils were horizontal, and always remained so, no matter the orientation of the cephalopod.

2.

Because the *Historia animalium* included illustrations—often of animals in their natural habitat—Gessner's approach to natural history was most unusual for sixteenth-century readers. Gessner acknowledges one of his main illustrators as Lucas Schan, an artist from Strasbourg, and also identifies the pictorial contributions of Olaus Magnus, Guillaume Rondelet, Pierre Belon, Ulisse Aldrovandi, and Albrecht Dürer. Their art was translated onto blocks of wood and carved by unknown craftsmen. The woodblocks were then used to "stamp" the illustrations in place between the blocks of text already printed on the pages.

During the past three decades, I have had ample opportunity to quote from Gessner's work (in translation, of course), and I have reproduced many of the marvelous illustrations that appear in these large, dense volumes. For example, my book *Monsters of the Sea* (Knopf, 1996) was concerned with whales, sharks, mermaids, giant squid, giant octopuses, and the Loch Ness Monster. Of these, only Nessie is missing from Gessner's volumes. There were a host of other creatures featured in Gessner that fell into no known category, such as *Simia marina*, the sea monkey.

Gessner's sea monkey illustration was taken directly from one drawn by Johannes Kentmann, a Dresden physician and naturalist who also identified it as *Simia marina*. As reproduced here, Gessner's *Simia marina* shows some resemblance to a seal (four "flippers"); a shark (a lot of teeth); an otter (four flippers and a long tail); and some sort of a fish (but there are no gills). Because Gessner wrote, "*Non pisces quid haec. Sed bestia cartilaginea* [Not fishes as such but cartilaginous beasts]," he obviously meant it to be a chimaera, a cartilaginous fish that is neither exactly a shark nor exactly a bony fish. In Greek mythology, the chimaera was a fire-breathing monster with the head of a lion, the body of a goat, and the tail of a serpent. Living chimaeras, of which there are some forty species, have large eyes and two dorsal fins, the first of which has a serrated, poison spine in front of it. Although they have multiple gill slits like sharks, the gill slits are covered by a plate known as the operculum (a flap) as in the bony fishes. They have a long, tapering tail, which accounts for one of their common names, "ratfish."

Despite its sometimes enigmatic inclusions, *Historia animalium* forms the solid basis for the study of ancient and modern zoology. Many of the known creatures (and several of the unreal ones) are meticulously described and illustrated in its five volumes. For an understanding of the history of zoology and a peek at some truly fascinating and five-hundred-year-old illustrations, there is no better historical guide than Conrad Gessner's *Historia animalium*.

2. One volume of the library's copy retains its 1551 binding with blind-stamping, sprinkled (decorative painted) vellum-covered wood boards, and brass and leather fore edge clasps—used to keep the boards from swelling and detaching from the text block. Intact, original fore edge clasps from this time are very rare.

3. The number and placement of the fins suggests that Gessner used a more or less accurate description, but the paddle-like snout is wrong.

4. Although Gessner called it *Simia marina* (sea monkey) this is probably a drawing of a dried specimen of a cartilaginous fish known as a chimaera. The prominent dorsal spine, big eye, and rat-like tail are characteristics of the chimaeras, but unlike sharks, they do not have visible gill slits.

5. The general shape of the hydra is reminiscent of a giant squid, except for some of the details, such as a crowned head on each of its seven "arms" and little clawed feet, but the Gessner illustration of a hydra might have been based on a contorted description of a beached specimen of *Architeuthis*.

6. The rhinoceros is taken directly from Albrecht Dürer's 1515 woodcut. Because Dürer never saw a rhino either, Gessner's copy reproduces all the original errors, such as a little horn protruding from its shoulder, armor plates, sleeves, pantaloons, scaly feet, and saw-like serrations on its tail.

Richard Ellis *is a research associate in the Division of Paleontology at the American Museum of Natural History.*

3.

4.

5.

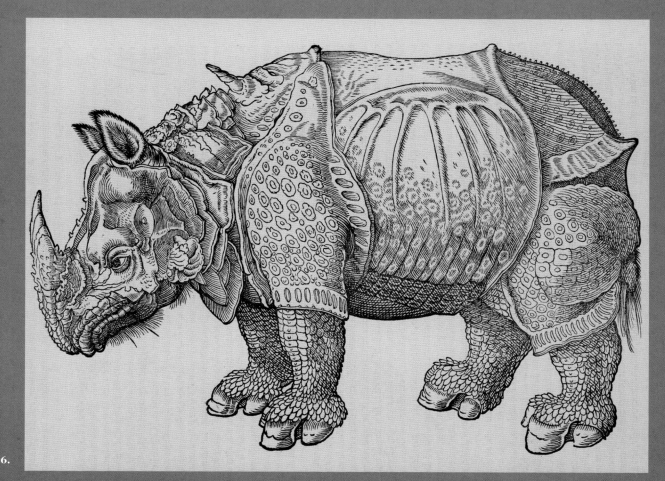

6.

First Glimpses of a New World

DAVID HURST THOMAS

Author
Theodor de Bry
(1528–1598)

Title
America

Imprint
Francoforti ad Moenum,
Typis I. Wecheli, . . .
1590–1634

Theodor de Bry was a Flemish goldsmith famed for his lavish engraved illustrations published in his highly influential *America*. Although born into wealth and status, de Bry felt it necessary to have a trade, so "I could fend for myself." When Spanish King Phillip II forced Protestants from the Netherlands, de Bry fled to Germany, where he opened a goldsmith's shop, but soon transformed himself into a skilled engraver. How de Bry came to create these works is an extraordinary tale, crisscrossing continents and encompassing war, colonization, and early, impressionable, and highly questionable views of the New World and its inhabitants.

Seeking new commissions to engrave and print, de Bry learned about an obscure series of paintings prepared by Jacques Le Moyne de Morgues, who had participated in an abortive attempt by French Huguenots to colonize Spanish Florida in the 1560s. Under the command of Réné Goulaine de Laudonnière, they established communications with native peoples, explored the mainland, and erected Fort Caroline on the south bank of the St. Johns River (along the future Florida–Georgia border). Their efforts were not viewed kindly by Spain.

In 1565, Pedro Menéndez de Avilés was dispatched by the Spanish Crown to solve the French problem. Setting up headquarters at St. Augustine, Florida, Menéndez moved quickly, capturing Fort Caroline and executing more than three hundred Frenchmen. Never again would France attack Spanish possessions along the eastern shores of North America.

On the day Menéndez attacked, Le Moyne escaped into the swamp and luckily encountered a French ship, the *Levrière*, aboard which he sailed to Europe. Blown off course to England, Le Moyne settled into London, where he lived in obscurity until 1586, when Laudonnière—who also survived the Fort Caroline massacre—published his account of the ill-fated French adventures in La Florida. In preparing the English translation of Laudonnière's account, Richard Hakluyt came across several color paintings rendered by James Morgues (a.k.a. the anglicized Jacques Le Moyne de Morgues), who had painted a number of scenes and episodes from his Florida experiences. Hakluyt raised the possibility of publication with Le Moyne, but they were unable to secure funding.

Doubtless in touch with Hakluyt, de Bry traveled to London in 1587 to purchase the Le Moyne pictures. A victim of religious persecution himself, he was anxious to publicize the sufferings of the Huguenots in the New World. Having already read Laudonnière's narrative, de Bry wanted to highlight the sufferings in a new, illustrated form. However, when Le Moyne refused to sell his paintings, de Bry turned his attention to another collection of paintings created by John White, one of the 107 English settlers who had accompanied Sir Walter Raleigh to establish

1. Timucuan deer hunters, depicted along the northeastern Florida coast in the 1560s, disguised themselves beneath masks with eyeholes and large deerskin capes, stalking their prey as they came to drink. After a successful ambush, the concealed archers skinned and butchered the carcasses with shell tools.

5

2.

Roanoke Colony in 1585. Appointed governor of Roanoke Island in 1587, White painted numerous watercolors documenting the American natives of Virginia, along with the local flora and fauna.

De Bry and his sons prepared twenty-three of White's paintings for his *Virginia* volume (published in 1590). After Le Moyne's death, de Bry purchased the paintings from his widow, and the next year de Bry's *Florida* book appeared, with forty-three engravings produced from Le Moyne's paintings (as well as two additional engravings based on White's watercolors). *Florida* and *Virginia* comprise but two of the thirteen books that make up *America*.

Several anthropologists have questioned the ethnographic accuracy of these images. It is unclear how much of de Bry's engravings were based directly on Le Moyne's firsthand observations, and how much derived from the engraver's imagination—or from details of Brazil's natives from other early French explorers. Even ignoring the stylized Greco-Roman bodies and the artificial European compositions—the French soldiers are shown wearing their helmets backward—the artifacts and activities shown cannot be taken as reliable representations of Timucuan or native Floridian life. The black drink ceremony depicted shows cups made of nautilus shells (unavailable in coastal Florida), and several of the Timucuan feather headdresses closely resemble those worn by Amazonian natives.

All shortcomings aside, for three centuries, these remarkable de Bry engravings defined the world's perceptions of American natives and provided seventeenth-century European readers with their first impressionable glimpse of the New World's inhabitants.

2. This remarkable image by John White (appointed governor of Roanoke Island in 1587) depicts the coastal Indians of Virginia. It is Europe's very first glimpse of America and its indigenous inhabitants. The fire basin amidships in the closest canoe was likely used for night fishing.

3. This graphic engraving shows a protected hunting blind on the left, concealing a watchman who called in teams of hunters to ambush alligators. After thrusting a sharpened pole into the alligator's mouth, they attacked his soft underbelly with clubs and spears.

4. This engraving probably shows Timucuan cooks preparing acorn meal or flour. In the background, men and women are grinding and picking acorns. At the left, they seem to be leaching out tannic acid with repeated water baths, after which the acorn meal is boiled in a large ceramic pot.

5. This mortuary scene shows grieving and fasting villagers around a burial mound. The deceased chief's black drink cup has been placed atop the grave, which is surrounded by arrows planted in the ground. In the background, the chief's house and council house have been set afire to destroy all his possessions.

David Hurst Thomas is a curator in the Division of Anthropology at the American Museum of Natural History.

3.

4.

5.

40

The Uranometria Star Atlas

MICHAEL SHARA

Author
Johannes Bayer
(1572–1625)

Title
Uranometria

(Measuring the sky)

Imprint
Augustae Vindelicorum:
Excudit Christophorus
Mangus, 1603

One of the great treasures of the American Museum of Natural History's library is its beautiful, early seventeenth-century star atlas *Uranometria*. Astronomers have been compiling star catalogs for millennia. Created in A.D. 120, Ptolomy's *Almagest* star catalog and description of the visible universe was the culmination of centuries of observing stars and was treated as dogma for 1,200 years. The *Uranometria* atlas of 1603 was a monumental leap forward from *Almagest*. Produced by lawyer and amateur astronomer Johannes Bayer, this state-of-the-art atlas (rather than a catalog which didn't illustrate stars' locations) was the first to cover the entire sky, contained 1,200 stars, and became the standard for all later atlases of the heavens. Rather than merely listing the stars—as in the *Almagest* catalog—*Uranometria* precisely mapped all of the visible, bright stars in the sky into sixty groupings, or constellations, that are exquisite works of art.

The *Uranometria* atlas was printed from engraved copper plates and bound in a vellum cover in 1603. The first forty-eight pages represent the forty-eight Ptolemaic constellations. The twelve southernmost constellations, unknown to Ptolemy, are on the forty-ninth page. This is followed by two planisphere illustrations, one mapping the stars in the entire Northern Hemisphere, and one mapping the stars in the Southern Hemisphere. A grid is superposed onto each image, allowing the reader to accurately determine the coordinates of any star to a small fraction of a degree—an unprecedented accuracy for its time.

The subject of each constellation is the artwork that dominates each plate. All of the classical constellations—from Andromeda, the chained Princess; Aries, the Ram; and Cygnus, the Swan, through Virgo, the Virgin; and Vulpecula, the Fox—are represented. The brightest star in every constellation is called Alpha, the next brightest is labeled Beta, and so on throughout the Greek alphabet. Thus, Betelgeuse—the brightest star in the constellation Orion and the eighth-brightest star in the night sky—was labeled Alpha Orionus by Bayer. Curiously, many of the human figures in *Uranometria* have their backs turned toward the reader. Betelgeuse occupies Orion the Hunter's left shoulder in Bayer's atlas, whereas Orion faces the reader on the right shoulder in most other atlases.

A few of the constellations and the artwork depicting them in *Uranometria* are so striking that we couldn't resist reproducing them for you on these pages— although choosing just a few was not easy. Serpentarius (the Serpent Holder), known since ancient times, is today referred to as Ophiuchus. A rather cheerful serpent with a forked tongue is grasped by a pensive-looking, bearded older man. The dark band running through the lower third of the image represents a 16-degree-wide path straddling the ecliptic. The ecliptic is an imaginary line tracing the apparent path of

1. Serpentarius

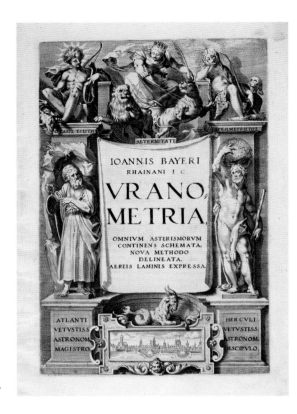

the Sun among the fixed stars, reflecting the Earth's true orbital motion about our host star. The pathway is the only part of the sky on which all of the classically known planets—Mercury, Venus, Mars, Jupiter, and Saturn, as well as the Sun and the Moon—ever appear.

Two jagged bands of darker texture run from the top left through the middle of the image. These represent the Milky Way, the diffuse band of light emitted by billions of stars too faint to be individually visible to the naked eye. I admit a fondness for Ophiuchus since it houses RS Ophiuchi, one of my favorite stars—a binary star system that undergoes vast explosions every few decades and that is about 5,000 light-years away from Earth.

We assume that Bayer's artist never saw a lion in the flesh, as Leo looks much more like an overgrown dog than a lion. Alpha Leonis, also known as Regulus, is at the heart of Leo. Our Sun and the vast majority of slowly spinning stars are almost perfectly spherical. Recent high-resolution images show that Regulus, one of the most rapidly rotating stars in the sky, is so distorted by its rapid spin that it's shaped like an egg. The ecliptic runs through Leo's feet, which is why this constellation is part of the zodiac. In addition, Ophiuchus-Serpentarius should be part of the zodiac, but, through no fault of his own, has fallen out of favor with current astrologers. One may have friends who proudly say that they are Geminis or Libras, but no one will own to being a Serpentarius.

Many of the constellations' stars do not form patterns that are even vaguely reminiscent of the people, animals, or things they're supposed to represent. Scorpius is a notable exception, and *Uranometria*'s threatening-looking scorpion makes this very clear. Perhaps next week, or next year, but certainly sometime in the next few hundred thousand years, the brilliant reddish star Antares, at the heart of Scorpius, will blow up as a supernova, becoming bright enough to be seen in broad daylight.

Bayer would be astounded and somewhat pleased to see his work updated as *Uranometria 2000*—the current, state-of-the-art star atlas that contains 280,000 stars, 26,000 galaxies, 2,000 star clusters, and nearly 2,000 nebulae (sites of star birth and death). Serious amateur astronomers use it to hunt for new comets, novae, and supernovae in distant galaxies. The original, luscious astrological images of the *Uranometria* are, unfortunately, gone, but it's apparent that *Uranometria*'s strong influence continues to be felt more than four hundred years later.

2. Alexander Mair (ca. 1562–1617) engraved *Uranometria*'s illustrations and title page. The allegorical figures seen here include Ptolemy and Hercules, flanking the title's text, and Apollo and Diana at the top, on either side of Eternity. A view of the city of Augsburg, where *Uranometria* was published, appears at the bottom beneath a figure of Capricorn.

3. Leo

4. Scorpius

5. Planisphere

Michael Shara *is a curator in the Astrophysics Department in the Division of Physical Sciences at the American Museum of Natural History.*

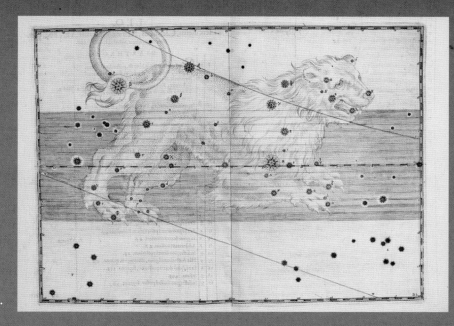

3.

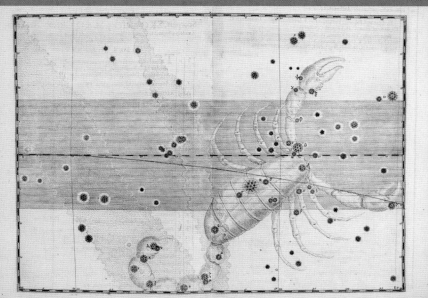

4.

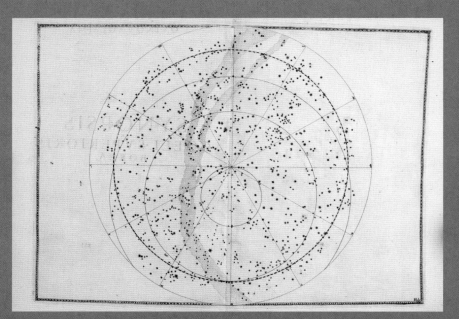

5.

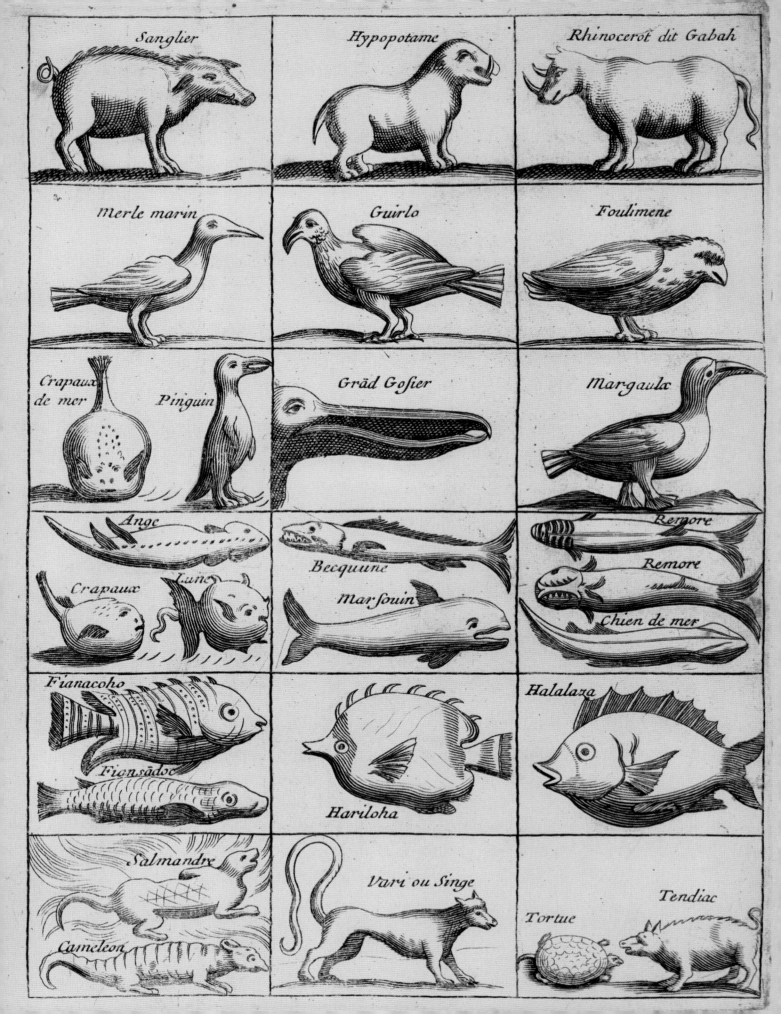

Sanglier

Hypopotame

Rhinocerot dit Gabah

Merle marin

Guirlo

Foulimene

Crapaux de mer

Pinguin

Grãd Gosier

Margaulæ

Ange

Crapaux

Lune

Becquune

Marsouin

Remore

Remore

Chien de mer

Fianacoho

Fignsãdoc

Hariloha

Halalaza

Salmandre

Cameleon

Vari ou Singe

Tortue

Tendiac

Flora, Fauna, and Fifangha: Madagascar by Flacourt

ALEX DE VOOGT

Author
Étienne de Flacourt
(1607–1660)

Title
*Histoire de la grande isle
Madagascar, avec une
relation de ce qui s'est passé és
années 1655, 1656 & 1657*

*(History of the great island of
Madagascar, with an account
of what happened in the years
1655, 1656 & 1657)*

Imprint
Troyes: N. Oudot, 1661

1. Flacourt's illustrations of
animals include the small
Madagascar hippopotamus (top
row, second from right).

The first edition of Étienne de Flacourt's *Histoire de la grande isle Madagascar* was published in 1658, authorized by French King Louis XIV and his consort. The second expanded edition contained in the American Museum of Natural History library collection was published by Oudot, and is dated 1661. Both editions are illustrated with woodblock plates of the flora, fauna, and people of Madagascar, as well as maps of the French settlement. The second edition was released after Flacourt's death—it is believed that his brother had taken charge of the book when Flacourt departed on what turned out to be his last trip to Madagascar on May 20, 1660.

Étienne de Flacourt was appointed governor of Madagascar in 1648, under the auspices of the French East India Company. He faced an increasingly hostile population that soon jeopardized the future of his encampment at Fort Dauphin as well as his efforts at trade with the locals. During the turbulent years that followed his arrival, he applied himself to a study of the island's natural wealth that would have a more promising outcome than his trade relations.

Since few had traveled to Madagascar, and even fewer had survived to tell the story, Flacourt's descriptions of natural history became a valuable resource. His illustrations feature the first record of the carnivorous plant *Nepenthes*, labeled *Anramitaco*, which can still be found today. There is also a rare record of the elephant bird, which he called *Vouron patra*, that "haunts the forest and that lays eggs like those of an ostrich"—it is one of few accounts of this now-extinct animal known today as *Aepyornis maximum*. Also illustrated is the small Madagascar hippo (*Hippopotamus madagascariensis*), which is now extinct. The giant lemur (*Megaladapis edwardsi*), known as *Tretretretre* in Malgache, was afraid of humans and like too many of the species Flacourt describes, no longer survives.

Beyond the natural richness of Madagascar, Flacourt also presents a history of French encounters with the indigenous peoples, as specifically mentioned in his title. The book features maps of Fort Dauphin that illustrate its ideal location for studying the flora and fauna of the island. More important, despite having been written centuries before ethnology matured as a science, Flacourt's anthropological descriptions of the Malagasy people are still valued and evaluated today. Researchers, anthropologists, and biologists—and there are several at the American Museum of Natural History who conduct research on this island—owe much to this early pioneer.

Among the varied illustrations is a seemingly simple drawing of a mancala game board consisting of four rows of eight holes. Flacourt added letters to the holes, which he referenced in his description of the rules—which happens to be the earliest recorded set of mancala rules, the first record of a four-row mancala game, and the earliest Western record of any mancala game. The letters that he added to his

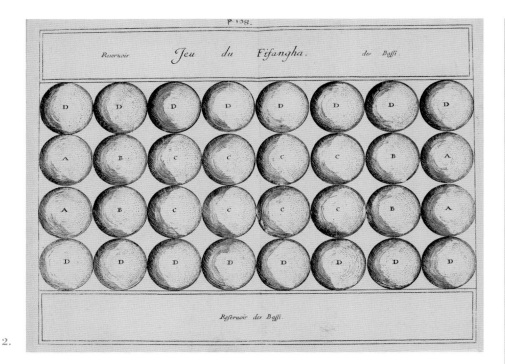

2. The mancala game *fifangha*, today known as *katra-be* in Madagascar and *bao* elsewhere in East Africa.

3. Slavery in Madagascar was present prior to the arrival of the French in the seventeenth century. This engraving shows a woman carried by slaves to the countryside accompanied by her husband standing on the right. The scene suggests that Flacourt recognized that there were differences in skin color between masters and slaves.

4. In his history of Madagascar, Flacourt includes five scenes depicting local people. This particular engraving shows two families. On the left, the "master of the village" and his wife are shown with a small child. On the right, a man from the Masikoro group with his wife and child are depicted with much darker skin, suggesting local differences in skin color, hairstyle, and general attire.

5. Fort Dauphin was strategically located near the sea. Despite the many conflicts with the local people, Flacourt was able to survey the neighboring areas for both flora and fauna.

drawing—in particular the holes marked A and B—refer to special rules associated with these holes and are also applied to the present-day games of *katra-be* in Madagascar and *bao* elsewhere in East Africa. Flacourt's record shows that these rules have a history of at least four hundred years. The game rules were not in the original manuscript, but were added later from memory and are included in the 1661 edition. The first edition did not present much more than a name of the game *fifangha,* described as "a game of the mind, similar to checkers or trictrac [backgammon]." The two pages in later editions that feature the rules are the perfect example of the detail for which his volumes on Madagascar have remained famous ever since.

In 1654, Flacourt sailed back home to France at the first opportunity of a ship that could take his men, and by 1658, he had completed his manuscript on the history and natural history of Madagascar. Flacourt departed for Madagascar once again to resume his administrative position on May 20, 1660, but never arrived. The ship was attacked by pirates and sunk, losing its cargo and killing Flacourt. Fort Dauphin was soon destroyed, too, by natural and human forces, before it was eventually abandoned altogether in 1674. Flacourt's work survived, however, and has been in print ever since.

Alex de Voogt is an assistant curator in the Division of Anthropology at the American Museum of Natural History.

3.

4.

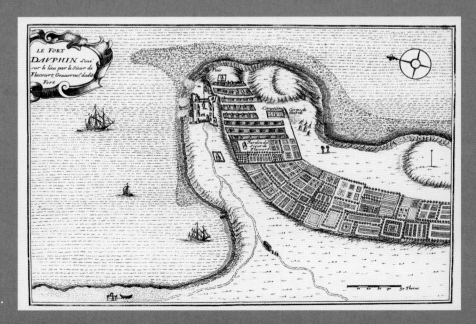

5.

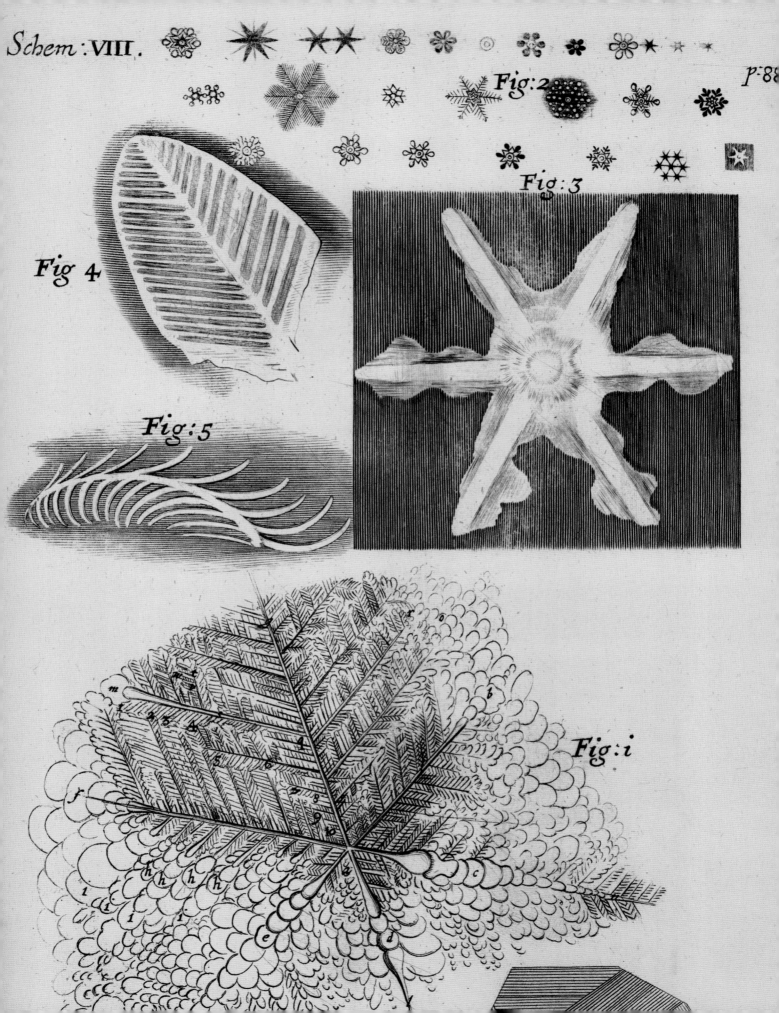

Fig:2

Fig:3

Fig 4

Fig:5

Fig:i

On the Strangeness of Hooke's Micrographia

DAVID KOHN

Author
Robert Hooke
(1635–1703)

Title
*Micrographia, or
some physiological
descriptions of minute bodies
made by magnifying glasses,
with observations and inquiries
thereupon*

Imprint
London: Printed for
J. Allestry, printer to the
Royal Society, 1667

Robert Hooke's *Micrographia* is an extraordinary book that invited its seventeenth-century readers to explore a new world invisible to the naked eye. Yet, it is also a strange book. The work features sixty brief essays based on Hooke's microscopic and telescopic observations, many exquisitely illustrated by engraved plates based on Hooke's own drawings. Some, like "On the Flea," achieve a sense of enormous magnification, as the fold-out plates are several times the size of the bound book. But the modern reader is struck by the heterogeneity of the objects that Hooke observed. To name just a handful: gravel in urine, petrified wood, blue mold, nettles' stings, bees' stings, feet of flies, teeth of snails, a louse, a bookworm, and stars in the Pleiades. One is reminded of a twisted version of those children's microscope sets that come complete with several innocuous prepared slides of feathers and hair, and bits of mica.

It is, in part, the heterogeneity of this collection of curious, often prickly, putrescent, and sharp objects that seems strange. For *Micrographia* was indeed written during the childhood—though not the infancy—of microscopy, when cultured adults could still be dazzled by the unanticipated worlds revealed in Hooke's stunning illustrations. *Micrographia* was one of the most popular scientific books of its age. British diarist Samuel Pepys hailed it as "the most ingenious book that ever I read." For the contemporary reader of *Micrographia*, its diverse curiosities were a coherent delight, an expansion of the senses, and a visual revelation.

But there is another strange element in *Micrographia*. Besides Hooke's direct observations of what he saw with his microscope, he also included much original theory and speculation in the essays accompanying his drawings. Yet there is no organized argument to the book. Although *Micrographia* and Newton's *Principia* are both masterpieces of the scientific revolution, they are exact opposites. True, Hooke's observations on cork brought him close to grasping the cellular organization of plants, and *Micrographia* inspired Leeuwenhoek's work in microscopy. He definitely both grasped that fossils are the remains of extinct beings and expressed an evolutionary view of life more than a century before Lamarck and Erasmus Darwin expanded on these notions. His work in optics anticipated Newton's studies on the diffraction of light passed through a prism. Yet in all Hooke's short pieces, most of the visionary ideas remain undeveloped.

The almost ephemeral quality of Hooke's science is bound up with the post he held in the Royal Society of London. The fledgling society, which in 1665 was but five years old, was eager to prove the merits and utility of science, and thereby justify the place of both science and the society within the new political and cultural order of the restoration monarchy—itself only five years old. One of the society's

1. "Urine by Freezing." Hooke describes geometric formations on frozen liquids, including (presumably his own) urine. A hypochondriac, who dosed himself with many dangerous substances, he also studied "gravel," i.e., passed stones in his urine.

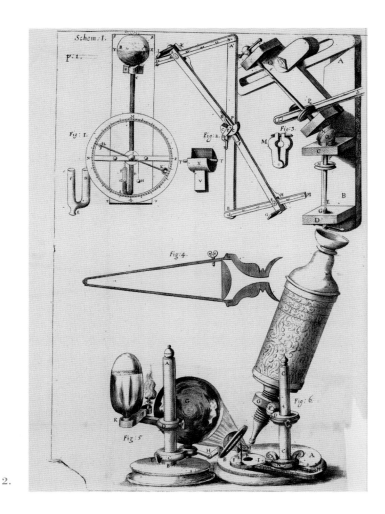

2.

2. Hooke's compound microscope had both an eyepiece lens
and an objective lens. For *Micrographia*, it was important that his
microscope was fitted with two
interchangeable lenses. Thus, he
was able to range from relatively
low power for views of whole
insects, like the flea, to high
power for details of snowflakes.

3. "Of the Schematisme." Hooke
termed the walled units he saw
in plant cells. He also questioned
how fluids or signals (as in the
sensitive plant at the bottom)
were transmitted if cells are
walled off from each other.

4. "Of Blue Mould." Hooke's
observations on objects such as
fossils and reproductive structures
in ferns, mosses, and fungi
launched daring speculations.
Here he even proposes that the
"All-wise Creator might . . .
directly design [that] a new
species can be the 'casual'
result of putrefaction."

5. "Of a Flea." *Micrographia*
includes many observations of
insects. Although these animals
are visible to the naked eye,
Hooke's detailed close-up observations of their external anatomy
are nothing less than spectacular,
and opened up new descriptive
dimensions in natural history.

*David Kohn is Director of
the Darwin Manuscripts
Project at the American
Museum of Natural History,
an associate in the museum's
Library, and Oxnam Professor
of the History of Science,
Emeritus, at Drew University.*

early moves was to appoint Robert Hooke as its Curator of Experiments in 1662.
Hooke was obliged—regularly and publicly—to demonstrate new experiments and
to design apparatus that furthered the experimental interests of the society's fellows.

Micrographia, the first book in English on microscopy, drew its material
from Hooke's public demonstrations. The Royal Society paid Hooke as Curator of
Experiments and supported the publication of his lectures because *Micrographia*
advanced a primary institutional imperative: to enhance the public's appreciation of
science. But Hooke's paid post placed him in the awkward social role of a servant
beholden to the society's fellows. Not only did the fellows' ceaseless demands deprive
him of time for sustained pursuit of any one line of research, but the society also constrained his inclination to adopt the role of a natural philosopher. The fellows voted
to renounce responsibility for any controversial positions in Hooke's essays; therefore, there was little social space for Hooke's ample originality to flourish. Perhaps
it is little wonder that Hooke became argumentative, boastful, and provoked prior-
ity disputes with contemporaries like Christiaan Huygens and Isaac Newton. But
Micrographia was Hooke's one great chance to shine. Perhaps this is why he filled
his essays with so much unripe fruit. We can grasp Hooke's historical moment if we
drop our modern understanding that science is not only a body of knowledge but also
an organized profession. Ultimately, the strangeness of *Micrographia* reflects the life
of a man who earned his living doing science, when science was not yet a profession.

Fig: I.

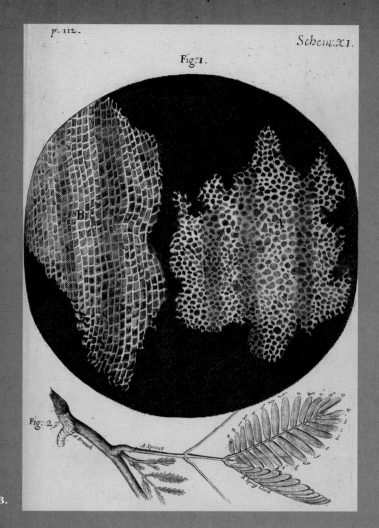

Fig: 2.

3.

Fig: I

Fig: 2.

4.

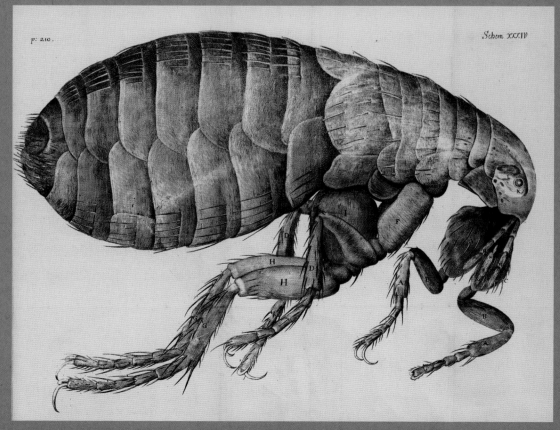

5.

Les Six
VOYAGES,
de Jean Baptiste
TAVERNIER,
Ecuyer Baron d'Aubonne,
en TURQVIE, en
PERSE, et aux
INDES.

The Buyer's Guide to India, Circa 1678

GEORGE E. HARLOW

Author
Jean-Baptiste Tavernier
(1605–1689)

Title
*Les six voyages de
Jean-Baptiste Tavernier, en
Turquie, en Perse et aux Indes*

*(The six voyages of Jean-
Baptiste Tavernier, through
Turkey into Persia and the
East Indies)*

Imprint
Amsterdam: Chez Johannes
van Someren, 1678

Stories of travel to the Orient became an important genre in early Western literature, as Orientalism[1] developed in Europe from the time of the Renaissance. An early example is Marco Polo's *Il Milione* (ca. 1299), known better as *The Travels of Marco Polo*. Not only was the East mysterious, rich, spectacular, and potentially dangerous, but it was also the source of precious gems—particularly diamonds from India. A noteworthy chapter in writings about (and commerce with) the Orient and trade in diamonds was *Les six voyages de Jean-Baptiste Tavernier, en Turquie, en Perse et aux Indes* (*The six voyages of Jean-Baptiste Tavernier, through Turkey into Persia and the East Indies*). Born in Paris, Jean-Baptiste Tavernier was the son of an engraver and geographer from Antwerp, Gabriel. Tavernier became a jeweler–merchant himself and had traveled internationally by the age of sixteen. He developed connections with the courts of Europe, and his travels included stays with Phillip Brenner, the viceroy of Hungary (1624–1629), and Charles I Gonzaga, the duke of Mantua (1629).

In 1631, Tavernier began his first voyage east to the Levant (Turkey), Persia (Iran), Baghdad, and places in between. His second voyage—commencing in 1638 with the assistance of Pere Joseph (agent to Cardinal Richelieu, first minister of France)—ventured farther east, where he visited the court of Shah Jehan, the Mughal emperor and owner of vast gem wealth from south Asia. These rich encounters led to additional voyages at the behest of Cardinal Mazarin, Richelieu's successor, and then Louis XIV of France to acquire diamonds for the crowns of Europe. Tavernier visited the major mines east of the Deccan plateau, including Kollur in the former kingdom of Golconda, Raolconda (Ramullakota), and Soumelpoor (Sampalpur).

Tavernier's second voyage provided him with a wealth of information on routes through the Orient, political histories, and spectacular diamonds. In fact, much of the historical knowledge of these diamond mining areas and the methods used in mining recorded in Western literature is from Tavernier's accounts in *Les six voyages*. Likewise, he describes the methods by which diamonds were evaluated in quality and value, currencies for exchange, and dealing with local rivalries. Over the course of his subsequent travels, he brought back more than twenty diamonds greater than twenty carats, and sold or gave many to Cardinal Mazarin (already owner of the Sancy and the Mirror of Portugal diamonds). The Tavernier Blue (112 carats, bought by Tavernier in 1642, and destined to become the Hope) was among twenty diamonds sold to Louis XIV in 1669, and figured in the book. His stories and diamonds enhanced the growing fascination and desire Europeans were developing for the Orient as well—as for the king of gems.

Tavernier's descriptions and drawings of fabulous diamonds from India are

1. European contact with Indian diamond miners is depicted in this frontispiece engraving from Tavernier's *Les six voyages* and evokes the exotic context.

21

2.

presented in Chapter XXII of Part 2[2] of *Les six voyages*, a diminutive work in two volumes, each barely 5 inches tall. Among the woodblock-executed illustrations are featured (1) the Great Mogul (279 $\frac{9}{16}$ carats[3]), which was recut and lost in history (although it's most likely now the Orlov displayed in the Kremlin); (2) the Grand Duke of Tuscany's diamond, which became the Florentine and the Austrian Yellow; (3) a 242 ½-carat stone seen in 1642 and now believed to be the Great Table; (4) a 157 ¼-carat diamond acquired by Tavernier and recut; (5) a diamond he acquired in 1653 of 63 ⅜ carats; and (6) two stones cleaved from a single 104-carat diamond.

Tavernier visited the treasury of Aurangzeb in 1665, on his last (sixth) completed voyage. One of the dazzling literary images in the book from that trip is that of the Peacock Throne of Shah Jehan, an elevated bed-like structure supported by four golden feet with a central cushion, all surmounted by a canopy embroidered with pearls and diamonds, and a fringe of pearl. Upon the top of the canopy stands a peacock, the body of beaten gold, a great ruby upon its breast, and with its tail spread covered with sapphires and colored stones. Some sources[4] mention diamond eyes on the Peacock Throne, which may have included the Koh-i-Noor (mountain of light, 105.6 carats) and Akbar Shah diamonds, although the latter's size—116 carats—may be more appropriate for the pendant that dangles adjacent to the throne cushion: "On the side of the throne, which is opposite the Court, there is to be seen a jewel consisting of a diamond of about 80 to 90 carats weight, with rubies and emeralds around it, and when the king is seated he has the jewel in full view."[5] Alternatively, this diadem may have been the Shah diamond. In any case, these stones enhance the image and the effect of Tavernier's observations.

Not satisfied with a life of wealth (he acquired the barony of Aubonne, near Geneva, after his fifth voyage) and sedentary style, in 1687 he left for Switzerland, then Berlin, Copenhagen, and finally Moscow on his way back to Persia. He died in Moscow in 1689, at the ripe age of eighty-four. Tavernier was the model of the inveterate traveler, as well as the most consequential diamond dealer of his age. His remarkable three-hundred-year-old book tells the stories of many significant gems that remain in the public mind today.

1. The term was given a pejorative meaning by Edward Said, which is not the intent here.
2. Tavernier, Jean-Baptiste. *The six voyages of Jean-Baptiste Tavernier, through Turkey into Persia and the East Indies*, English translation, London, 1678.
3. Carats are as written in Tavernier's original text, not corrected to current metric standards.
4. Streeter, Edwin W. *The Great Diamonds of the World*, George Bell & Sons, London, second edition, 1882.
5. Tavernier, J.-B. Op. cit.

2. The two volumes of *Les six voyages* were small enough to be easily carried while on a reader's own travels. The spines of the full leather bindings, in the French style of the day, are gilt with attached leather labels.

3. A group of twenty select diamonds sold by Tavernier to Louis XIV of France and, to the far right, three rough rubies, each shown from front and back sides.

4. Drawings of the diamonds described in the text. Number 1 is the Great Mogul.

5. Symbols of the Dutch East India Company, *Vereenigde Oost-Indische Compagnie*, VOC, "United East India Company," which were stamped on either side of silver coins (*reales*) and which the Dutch used in trade from their colonial capital in Batavia (Jakarta).

George E. Harlow is a curator in the Earth and Planetary Science Department in the Division of Physical Sciences at the American Museum of Natural History.

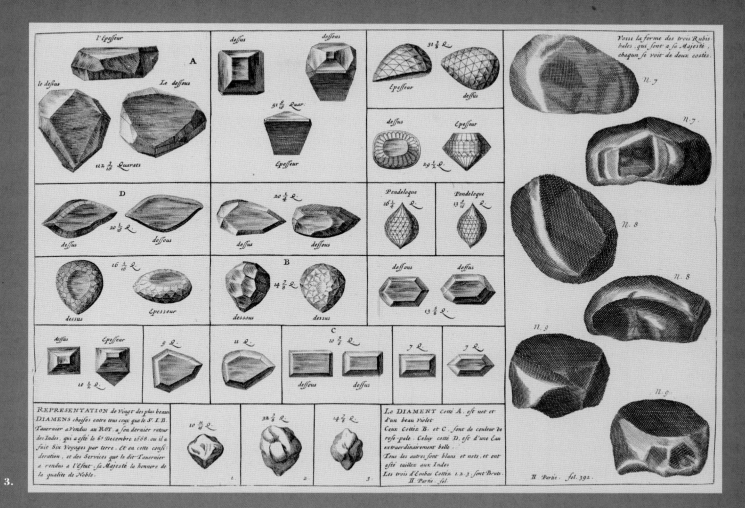

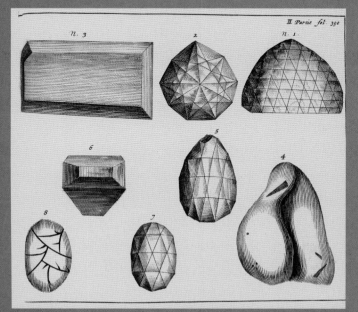

3.

4.

5.

Made Merian

PAULA SCHRYNEMAKERS

Author
Maria Sibylla Merian
(1647–1717)

Title
*Metamorphosis insectorum
Surinamensium,* or
*Over de voortteeling en won-
derbaerlyke veranderlingen
der Surinaemsche insecten . . .*

*(Metamorphosis of the insects
of Surinam,* or
*On the procreation and
wonderful changes of the
insects of Surinam . . .)*

Imprint
Amsterdam: Joannes
Oosterwyk, 1719

1. Engraved by Pieter Sluyter (1675–1713), this well-known Merian plate depicts a pineapple with a caterpillar, its chrysalis and butterfly forms, and a red, winged insect. The translation reads, "This is the ripe pine, in the crown of the fruit is drawn a little red vermin, small chrysalis, which devours the cochineal."

This caterpillar is of a beautiful yellow and red under the belly, and has a large flame coloured stripe upon the tail, it inhabits the Citron, and eats the boughs therof . . . it produced a large moth, which was gold coloured and striated with white, both in the upper and under the wings, on each which it had a bright spot shining like icing glass surrounded with a white circle, and round that with a black one so that it looks like a looking glass set in a case, and those who are of that opinion call the caterpillar the spiegeldragger, or the looking glass bearer.

From this excerpt, the translation of the sixty-fifth plate (see figure 5) of *Metamorphosis insectorum Surinamensium,* it is easy to see why Maria Sibylla Merian was one of the most influential naturalists of her day. Her uncomplicated and direct, descriptive narratives perfectly complement her scientifically beautiful renderings of insect metamorphoses. She brilliantly conveys the passage of time by organizing each image around the appropriate host plant and depicting every stage of metamorphosis from egg, to caterpillar, to adult. The library of the American Museum of Natural History possesses an edition of her *Metamorphosis* that has a unique characteristic: each plate in this 1719 Dutch edition is interleaved with pages bearing handwritten eighteenth-century English translations of the text. The translator's identity remains a mystery.

Although the original binding of the library's edition of *Metamorphosis* is long gone, what remains is a poetically written text with seventy-two sumptuously rendered, hand-colored engravings. Included in this total are twelve additional plates and a frontispiece that were not in the 1705 first edition. Ten plates were provided by the author's daughters, from material they inherited after Merian's death, and two were supplied by fellow naturalist Albert Seba. Indeed, Merian's contribution to the field of entomology was so important at the time that the engraved, allegorical frontispiece of Pieter Cramer's seminal work on butterflies, *Die Uitlandische Kapellen* (1779–1782), includes a stack of books, one of whose spines clearly has Merian's name written on it. This is no small feat for a woman in her day.

A seventeenth-century painter, engraver, publisher, naturalist, and master observer, Maria Sibylla Merian was born in 1647, in Frankfurt, Germany. Being the daughter of Matthaus Merian the Elder, an established engraver and publisher, one could see where her passion for observation and detail was born. Anecdotally speaking, her father predicted that one day his daughter would be the member of the family to make the Merian name famous. Merian the Elder died when Maria was just three, and her mother married Jacob Marell, a still-life painter and copper engraver. In a time when girls were not encouraged to flourish or think for themselves, Marell would impart his skills to the young Maria and would become the father who was her

2.

greatest influence and teacher. Many biographies of Merian have credited her with saying that she had begun her observations of nature when she was just thirteen. "From my youth onward I have been concerned with the study of insects. . . . This led me to collect all . . . and to work at my painter's art so that I could sketch them from life and represent them in life-like colors."

In 1665, Merian married Johann Andreas Graff, a favorite pupil of Marell, and a painter and engraver in his own right. Following her conversion to Labadism, a Protestant religious community movement, they divorced after he was refused admittance to the group. In 1683, Cornelius van Sommelsdyk, a sympathizer to the Labadist movement, left Holland to become the governor of Suriname. A body of Labadists followed him there and sought asylum after the surrender of New York by the Dutch to the English. Merian's older daughter, Johanna Helena, also moved to Suriname with her merchant husband.

In 1699, while living in Holland, Merian was inspired by the tropical specimens she saw during her visits to museums, private collections, and cabinets of curiosities, as well as the recently founded Botanical Gardens in Amsterdam, and in particular, by a specimen she saw that was brought from Suriname. So moved was she that she set out with her younger daughter, Dorothea, on an extended and expensive journey.

At fifty-two and twenty-one years of age, they set out, unaccompanied by a male chaperone, on a profound and spiritual journey to exotic Suriname. They lived in the house of the now-late Governor van Sommelsdyk and utilized the services of the local peoples and slaves, or as she referred to them, "myne . . . Indiaan and . . . Slaven."

> In January, 1701, I set out into the forest of Suriname to see what I could discover. Searching about, I found this graceful red blossom in the tree; neither the name nor the qualities of this tree are known to the inhabitants of this country. Here I came upon a beautiful and very large red caterpillar with three blue beads on each segment and a black feather protruding from each of the beads.

Merian spent two remarkably fruitful years in Suriname, painstakingly recording and painting insect and plant life. The culmination of this passion would lead her to publish *Metamorphosis*, her most important work. It was originally published in Amsterdam, in Dutch and Latin, in a folio edition of sixty copper plates, with the buyer having the choice of black-and-white or hand-colored engravings. In advertising copy issued for the book, other naturalists would go on to say that Merian's art was "[t]he most beautiful work ever painted in America."

Two years after her mother's death, Dorothea continued her mother's legacy to the field of entomology by selling the *Metamorphosis* plates to a Dutch publisher, who would reissue a new edition of the folio—with the additional twelve plates mentioned earlier—in 1719.

2. The richly illustrated baroque frontispiece in *Metamorphosis insectorum Surinamensium*, engraved by Frederik Ottens, purports to depict Merian with a group of cherubic assistants in the process of preparing specimens for her book.

3. This plate features the passion flower, so named for either its aphrodisiac qualities, or for the legend that the flower's parts symbolize the Passion of Christ. Merian masterfully captures the fluid tendrils of the flower, the ripeness of the fruit, an eager winged insect, and the stages of the moth metamorphosis.

4. This richly colored plate depicts a branch of the coral bean tree, with caterpillars and chrysalis, and two emperor moths flittering around it. Through the translation, Merian describes the caterpillar as "yellow striated with black and armed with six spikes."

5. The American Museum of Natural History copy of this work is unique. Originally, the Dutch text faced the image from the opposing page. In this copy, an earlier owner of the volume translated and transcribed the text and then inserted the pages between the plates and the Dutch text so that the English translations faced the image. Merian describes the citron bough with the moth metamorphosis of the "caterpillar spiegeldragger" or the "looking glass bearer."

Paula Schrynemakers is a rare books conservator who works on grant-funded projects in the Library's Conservation Lab at the American Museum of Natural History.

3.

4.

5.

Explanation of y 63.th Plate

This Caterpillar is of a beautifull yellow colour & red under y Belly & has a
large Plumm coloured Stripe upon y back it inhabits y Colours & Cells of Boughs
thereof, but is but seldome found, On y 25.th Feb. it Spun a Bag & changed into
a Chrysalis the Threads of y Bag were of such Silk as excells that of y Silk worms
both in Splendor & thickness, & it is to be lamented, that so few of these Caterpillars
are found & I am certain that great Profit might be made by them, if they
could be bred as easily as other Caterpillars, tho I believe no one ever yet
attempted it. On y 25.th March it produced a Large Moth which was Gold coloured
& red Streaked with white, both in y upper & under Wings, on each of which it had
a bright spot shining like Iseing Glass surrounded with a white Circle, & round
that with a black one, so that it looks like a Looking Glass set in a Case, & those
who were of that Opinion call y Caterpillars Spiegeldragger, or the Looking
Glass bearer.

Fig. 2.

Fig. 4.

Fig. 1.

The Apothecary's Cabinet

ROBERT S. VOSS

Author
Albert Seba
(1665–1736)

Title
*Locupletissimi rerum
naturalium thesauri accurata
descriptio, et iconibus
artificiosissimis expressio per
universam physices historiam*

*(The richest treasures of the
natural world accurately
described, and represented
with the most skillfully
rendered images for a general
history of natural science, or
Thesaurus)*

Imprint
Amstelaedami: apud J.
Weststenium, . . . 1734–1765

1. Some of the specimens in Seba's cabinet were obviously fakes. This hydra may have been purchased by some inebriated sailor.

Albert Seba was a wealthy Dutch apothecary and collector, whose private natural history museum in Amsterdam was one of the largest and most remarkable of its day. A childhood interest in collecting stones, shells, plants, and animals persisted to adulthood, and commercial success in middle age enabled him to indulge his passion to the fullest. Although Seba is not known to have traveled outside of Europe, eighteenth-century Amsterdam was one of the great world centers of maritime trade, and the Dutch overseas trading empire then included colonies in Africa, Asia, South America, and the East and West Indies. As an apothecary in an age when nostrums were frequently compounded from exotic materials, Seba had an extensive foreign correspondence that he used to obtain rare and valuable specimens, and we know from contemporary accounts that he visited returning ships in the harbor with medicaments for their sick and exhausted crews, perhaps sometimes trading curatives for curiosities. These commercial connections doubtless explain the many zoological novelties in Seba's collections, and their exceptional interest for contemporary scientists.

Seba made two large collections, the first of which was sold to Peter the Great when the czar visited Amsterdam in 1717. Seba immediately began to gather a second collection that grew apace and that was studied by Carl Linnaeus in 1735. By then, Seba's plans to produce a virtual museum—a series of magnificently illustrated volumes depicting all of his specimens for the delectation of well-heeled bibliophiles—were well at hand. Seba contracted for the production of this ambitious and unprecedented work in 1731; the first volume appeared in 1734 and the second appeared in 1735. Unfortunately, Seba died the following year, and disputes among his heirs about how to finance the publication of the remaining volumes resulted in a long delay. Thus, the third volume did not appear until 1759, and the fourth and final volume was not published until 1765.

In all, Seba's *Thesaurus* (as it is commonly known in lieu of its complete Latin title) comprises 449 folio plates by at least ten different artists. The accompanying text appeared in two versions, one in Latin and Dutch, the other in Latin and French. Subscribers had the option of purchasing each volume for 40 guilders with uncolored plates, or for 200 guilders with colored plates. The American Museum of Natural History's set—bound in elaborately tooled and gilded red morocco—is one of only a few known copies with uncolored plates. Although colored copies provide important information about the pigmentation of Seba's specimens, the uncolored plates in the museum's copy allow us to appreciate the exceptional quality of the copperplate engravings, the fine details of which are unobscured by color overlays. For many species, these were the first accurate renditions to appear in print.

2.

The enduring scientific value of Seba's *Thesaurus* rests in the fact that the illustrated specimens include the type (original) specimens of many species first described by Linnaeus and other eighteenth-century taxonomists. Type specimens are crucially important for taxonomy because they determine the application of scientific names when published descriptions of species are inadequate or inaccurate. Because Seba's collection was broken up and sold at auction after his death, many specimens were subsequently lost. In some cases, plates in the *Thesaurus* are the only basis for identifying species that were ambiguously described by Linnaeus. In other cases, Seba's illustrations have been used to recognize the original specimens, which have been rediscovered from time to time in various parts of Europe. Oldfield Thomas, for example, found several dozen mammals preserved in old-fashioned glass jars that were gathering dust in a neglected British Museum storeroom in 1911. Comparisons with plates in the first two volumes of the *Thesaurus* convinced Thomas that the specimens were part of Seba's second collection and are, therefore, types of several Linnaean species.

For most non-taxonomists, however, Seba's plates are chiefly remarkable for their other qualities: dramatic composition, strange juxtaposition, unexpected pathos, and sheer whimsicality. Enormous serpents writhe above seemingly oblivious armadillos in one plate; an opossum delicately sniffs a floral nosegay in another; a fetal elephant appears to slumber peacefully next to a human fetus suspended in an alcohol-filled jar. Accurately rendered, most of the animals depicted in Seba's plates can be identified to species, but others seem to have emerged incongruously from some medieval bestiary: a seven-headed hydra, for example, perhaps stitched together from animal parts by a huckster in some distant port and sold to a credulous sailor, eventually finding a home in Seba's wonderful cabinet.

Robert S. Voss *is a curator in the Mammalogy Department in the Division of Vertebrate Zoology at the American Museum of Natural History.*

ALBERTVS SEBA, ETZELA OOSTFRISIVS
Pharmacopoeus Amstelaedamenſis
ACAD: CAESAR: LEOPOLDINO CAROLINAE NAT: CVRIOS: COLLEGA XENOCRATES DICTVS:
SOCIET: REG: ANGLICANAE. et ACAD: SCIENTIAR: BONONIENSIS INSTITVTVS SODALIS.
AETATIS LXVI ANNO CIƆIƆCCXXXI.

3.

4.

5.

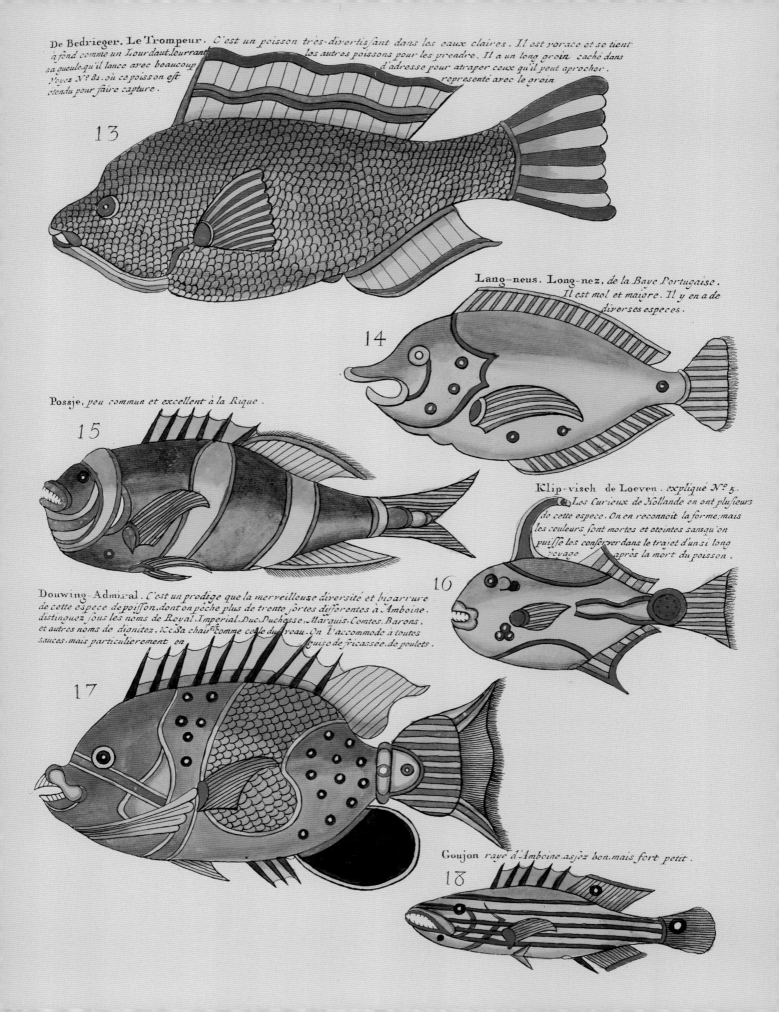

De Bedrieger. Le Trompeur. C'est un poisson très-divertissant dans les eaux claires. Il est vorace et se tient à fond comme un Lourdaut, leurrant les autres poissons pour les prendre. Il a un long groin caché dans sa gueule, qu'il lance avec beaucoup d'adresse pour atraper ceux qu'il peut aprocher. Voyez N.º 81. où ce poisson est représenté avec le groin étendu pour faire capture.

13

Lang-neus. Long-nez, de la Baye Portugaise. Il est mol et maigre. Il y en a de diverses especes.

14

Possje, peu commun et excellent à la Rique.

15

Klip-visch de Loeven. expliqué N.º 5. Les Curieux de Hollande en ont plusieurs de cette espece. On en reconnoit la forme, mais les couleurs sont mortes et eteintes sans qu'on puisse les conserver dans le trajet d'un si long voyage après la mort du poisson.

16

Douwing-Admiral. C'est un prodige que la merveilleuse diversité et bigarrure de cette espece de poisson, dont on pêche plus de trente sortes differentes à Amboine. distinguez sous les noms de Royal. Imperial. Duc. Duchesse. Marquis. Comtes. Barons et autres noms de dignitez. &c Sa chair comme celle du veau. On l'accommode à toutes sauces, mais particulierement en guise de fricassée de poulets.

17

Goujon rayé d'Amboine, asséz bon, mais fort petit.

18

Louis Renard and His Book of Extraordinary Creatures

MAI QARAMAN REITMEYER

Author
Louis Renard
(1678–1746)

Title
Poissons, écrevisses et crabes,
de diverses couleurs et
figures extraordinaires, que
l'on trouve autour des isles
Moluques et sur les côtes des
terres australes

(Fishes, crayfishes and crabs of
diverse colors and extraordinary
forms, which are found around
the islands of the Moluccas and
on the coasts of southern lands)

Imprint
Amsterdam: Chez Reinier &
Josué Ottens, 1754

1. Although there are many coloration and anatomical errors in these drawings, many of the specimens depicted can be identified as actual animals. In this plate, all the specimens can be identified to genus, and some even to species.

*P*oissons, écrevisses et crabes was first published by Louis Renard in 1718 or 1719, when little was known of East Indian marine fauna. It is the earliest known work on fishes to be published in color and an important part of the scientific literature of the eighteenth century, the new Age of Enlightenment.

Louis Renard was born in France circa 1678, to a Huguenot family that eventually fled to the Netherlands to escape religious persecution. Renard settled in Amsterdam in 1699, and became a member of the Walloon (French Reformed) Church. Unfortunately, not much is known about his early childhood or education. In 1703, he became a citizen of Amsterdam and, in the same year, married Germaine de la Feuille. Under the influence of his father-in-law, Daniel de la Feuille, Renard established himself as a book dealer and publisher. Between 1704 and 1724, a number of works were published under Renard's name, including publications dealing with current events and large-format atlases for which he supplied the text, including a maritime atlas "of all parts of the world." However, his *Poissons, écrevisses et crabes* was by far his most substantial publication.

This two-volume work, whose title translates to *Fishes, crayfishes and crabs, of diverse colors and extraordinary forms, which are found around the islands of the Moluccas and on the coasts of southern lands*, consists of one hundred plates comprising 460 hand-colored copper engravings. Each part bears the half title, or subtitle, *Histoire naturelle des rares curiositez de la mer des Indes (Natural history of the rarest curiosities of the seas of the indies)*, which is also a name by which this work is widely known.

Curiously, in the dedication, Renard identifies himself as a "secret agent on behalf of the British Crown." Primarily employed by George I and George II, his duties included searching ships leaving Amsterdam to prevent arms from reaching James Stuart, the Roman Catholic "Old Pretender" to the British throne—thereby helping to guarantee Protestant succession. While his role was hardly "secret," he may have thought that revealing this would garner attention and also help sell his books.

Three editions of this book are known. Renard published the first volume in 1718 or 1719, and only sixteen copies of this edition are known. The second edition, published by Reinier and Ottens in Amsterdam in 1754, is nearly identical to the first. This version is only slightly more accessible with thirty-four known copies, including the American Museum of Natural History's copy, which is bound together in one volume. The third and rarest edition is from 1782, by Abraham van Paddenburg and Willem Holtrop, Utrecht and Amsterdam. Only six copies are known. This edition was never completed—accounting for its extreme rarity.

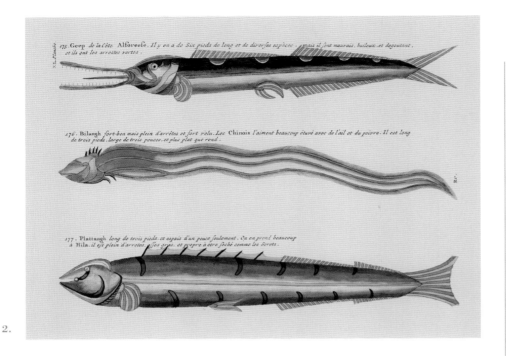

175. Geep de la Côte Alforeese. Il y en a de Six pieds de long et de diverses espèces : mais ils sont mauvais, huileux, et dégoutant, et ils ont les arrestes vertes.

176. Bilangh fort-bon mais plein d'arrêtes et fort velu. Les Chinois l'aiment beaucoup étuvé avec de l'ail et du poivre. Il est long de trois pieds, large de trois pouces, et plus plat que rond.

177. Plattangh long de trois pieds, et espais d'un pouce seulement. On en prend beaucoup à Hila, il est plein d'arrestes, et fort propre à être séché comme les Sorets.

2.

Almost all of the illustrations represent tropical species of the East Indies, including 415 fishes and forty-one crustaceans. Unlike other naturalists, Renard never left the Netherlands to observe and collect the species depicted in these volumes. Rather, as he mentions in the introduction, he copied drawings belonging to both Baltazar Coyett, the Dutch governor of Ambon (Molucca Islands), and Coyett's successor, Adriaen Van der Stel. Both governors, employees of the Dutch East India Company, had a keen interest in natural history and commissioned drawings of the local flora and fauna from local artists. A Dutch artist named Samuel Fallours, a soldier with the Dutch East India Company at Ambon, was responsible for many of these drawings. Due to a high demand for all matter of "curiosities," Fallours hired native artists to make multiple copies of his work, which he then sold to European collectors. Fallours also copied drawings of other artists, resulting in several sets of similar drawings that became the basis of several eighteenth-century publications in Holland, including Renard's *Poissons*.

Many of the species represented in *Poissons* had been known before to Europeans as dried or preserved specimens, lacking their natural colors—which rapidly fade upon death. As a result, Renard, who was part of a growing movement whereby scientific inquiry was based on direct observation and reason, felt it necessary to provide testimony to his work in case anyone questioned the brilliant colors depicted in the original drawings. Despite his assertions, none of the illustrations in this work is a completely accurate representation of any living species, and most, if not all, of the brief descriptions are nothing more than fabrications.

While most of the engravings are scientifically inaccurate, they are not just fantasy. A thorough examination of his work, performed by ichthyologist Theodore W. Pietsch in the late twentieth century, found that only approximately nine percent of the illustrations fall into a category that might be referred to as truly fantastical. Thus, Pietsch asserts that "to cast the work off as being without scientific merit is to greatly underestimate its value" as it "gives us an intriguing glimpse of what science was like in the late seventeenth and early eighteenth centuries."

2. Some of the specimens are described by their edibility and are accompanied by recipes. For example, the bliangh (bandfish) is described as "very good, but full of bones and very hairy. The Chinese like it very much when steamed with garlic and pepper."

3. The only text in this work is the engraved descriptions that appear on the plates themselves. Examples of text engraved on the same plate with illustrations is fairly uncommon, as the engraver would have had to engrave the text into the copper plate in reverse.

4. This illustration is easily identified as a longhorn cowfish (*Lactoria cornuta*) by the two pairs of longhorns like those of a cow or bull. Like all species in this family, it also has hexagonal or honeycomb-patterned scales that form the solid, box-like carapace from which the fins and tail protrude.

5. Despite Renard's testimony to the authenticity of the work, it is obvious that many of the illustrations were exaggerated. One can see small human faces depicted in the carapaces of the crabs.

6. The common names of species appearing in these volumes come from a mixture of several languages including Dutch, French, Malay, and other native local dialects.

Mai Qaraman Reitmeyer *is the Research Services Librarian in the Research Library at the American Museum of Natural History.*

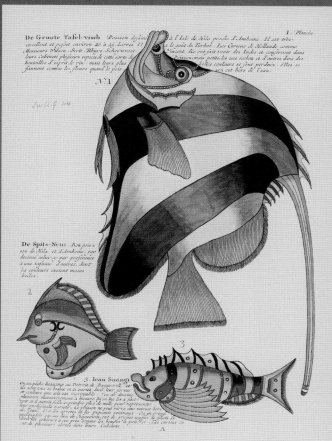

De Groote Tafel-visch *Poisson dessiné ... à l'Isle de Nila proche d'Amboine. Il est très-*
excellent et pesoit environ 20 à 25. Livres. ...
Messieurs d'Idem, Scott. Rhur, Schienvies ... à le sout du Torbot. Les Curieux de Hollande comme
leurs cabinets plusieurs espèce de cette sorte se ... Vincent &c ont fait venir des Indes et conservent dans
bouteilles d'esprit de vin: mais leurs plus ... Poisson: mais petits. Ils une espèce et d'autres dans des
fannent comme les fleurs quand le pois ... belles couleurs se sont perdues. Elles se
... son est hors de l'eau.

N°1

De Spits-Neus. *Bon pois-*
son de Nila, et d'Amboine: par
dessine celui-ce par préférence
à une infinité d'autres, dont
les couleurs etoient moins
belles

2

3. Ican Suangi
On en pêche beaucoup au Détroit de Banneveld: et
... son le boüne en le variété dans leur jonnas
... couleurs que cela est incroiable. L'on ai dessine
... plusieurs successivement à mesure qu'on les a pris ...
que ai autre fallu reprendre plus de mille pour represen-...
leur prochende naturel: le poisson ne peut vivre une minau hors ...
de l'eau. Il a des arretes les piquans venimeux: il a grand ...
... vui au lieu de Nageoires: car de arretes aigües les fillets de ...
... couleurs à un pied longeur des bouches à pointe. Les curieux en ...
... de plusieurs sorts dans leurs Cabinets.

A

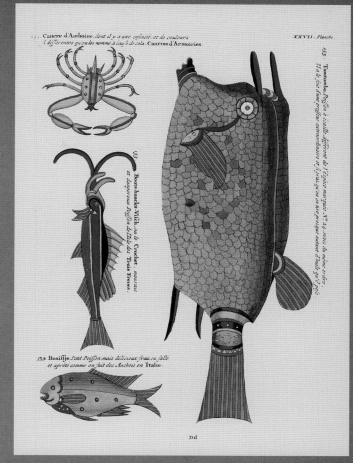

4

132. Cancre d'Amboine *dont il y a une infinité, et de couleurs*
à différentes qu'on les nomme à cause de cela. Cancres d'Armoiries

XXVII. Planche.

133. Boots-haacks-Vich, ou le Crochet, *mauvais*
et dangereux Poisson de l'Isle des Trois Freres.

435 Toutonbo, *Poisson à écaille, différent de l'espèce marquée N°. 43, mais du même ordre.*
Il a le foie d'une profiteur extraordinaire et se réduit en une presque autant d'huile qu'il pese.

Dd

134. Benilije. *Petit Poisson: mais délicieux frais ou sallé*
et apprète comme on fait des Anchois en Italie.

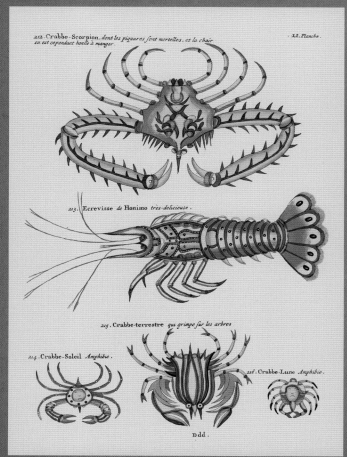

5

212. Crabbe-Scorpion. *dont les piqueures sont mortelles, et la chair*
en est cependant bonne à manger

LL. Planche.

213. Ecrevisse de Honimo *très-delicieuse.*

215. Crabbe-terrestre *qui grimpe sur les arbres*

214. Crabbe-Soleil *Amphibie.*

216. Crabbe-Lune *Amphibie.*

Ddd.

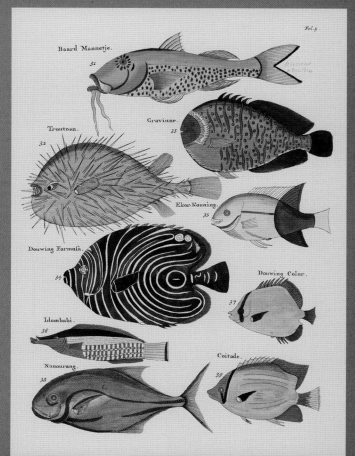

Fol. 5

Baard Mannetje.
31

Troutoen.
32

Gravinne.
33

Ekor Kouning.
35

Douwing Formosa.
34

Douwing Color.
37

Idombabi.
36

Nanourang.
38

Coitade.
39

ADMIRANDA T...
LEVIVM SPECTACVLA
RERVM

Rösel von Rosenhof and His Natural History of Frogs

DARREL FROST

Author

August Johann Rösel von
Rosenhof (1705–1759)

Title

*Historia naturalis ranarum
nostratium in qua omnes
earum proprietates, praesertim
quae ad generationem ipsarum
pertinent, fusius enarrantur.*

*(Natural history of the native
frogs in which all things
peculiar to them, especially
those that pertain to their
reproduction, are extensively
explained)*

Imprint

Nuremberg: Johann Joseph
Fleischmann, 1758

1. In the foreground of the engraved and hand-colored frontispiece, one finds the fire newt (*Salamandra salamandra*); the sand lizard (*Lacerta agilis*) on the rose's stem; the European tree frog (*Hyla arborea*) hanging from the rose bush; two green frogs (*Pelophylax lessonae*) and a brown frog (*Rana temporaria*) in the water; and a natterjack toad (*Epidalea calamita*) in the shadow of a Latin-inscribed stone which reads "The natural history of our country's frogs."

August Johann Rösel von Rosenhof stands out among early naturalists and natural history artists for his detailed observations and highly accurate illustrations. Indeed, his *Historia naturalis ranarum nostratium (Natural history of the native frogs)* remains one of the most beautifully illustrated natural history books of all time. He was born into a noble Austrian family who had relocated to the Nuremberg area in the sixteenth century during the Reformation and who had been raised again to the minor nobility by Holy Roman Emperor Ferdinand II in 1628 for services to the crown. This meant that Rösel was entitled to use the "von Rosenhof" as part of his name, although he did not do so until the last six years of his life.

August Johann Rösel was born near Arnstadt in the German principality of Arnstadt-Schwarzburg. His grandfather, Franz Rösel, was a painter of animals and landscapes, as was his uncle, Wilhelm Rösel. When August was orphaned at a young age, his godmother, the princess Augusta Dorothea von Arnstadt-Schwarzburg, took over responsibility for his education. After 1720, once she saw artistic talent in the young man, she sent him for training to his uncle, Wilhelm Rösel von Rosenhof, already a well-known artist. Subsequently, in 1724, August was apprenticed for two years to Johan Daniel Preisler in Nuremberg for advanced artistic training. Following this, in 1726, he became a painter of portraits and miniatures to the Danish Court in Copenhagen for two years, after which (in 1728) he returned to Nuremberg.

It was in Nuremberg at this time that he was introduced to Maria Sibylla Merian's richly illustrated book, *Metamorphosis insectorum Surinamensium* (1705), which inspired him to study German insect species and produce a similar work. This fascination with the natural world—particularly with the natural history of insects, but also of amphibians and reptiles—dominated the rest of his life.

In 1737, August married Elisabeth Maria, the daughter of the surgeon, physiologist, and poet Michael Bertram Rosa. August's artistic talent provided him a comfortable living from painting, and he used his remaining time to observe insects, amphibians, and reptiles in nature. He collected eggs and larvae of both insects and amphibians in order to study their development and metamorphoses. His detailed observations, made more useful by their beautiful accompanying illustrations, were published in two large multipart volumes—one on insects, the other on frogs.

In 1740, the first part—*Der monatlich-herausgegeben Insecten-Belustigung*—appeared, with four additional parts following. The final one was published posthumously in 1761. The work was noted not only for the beautiful illustrations, but also for the scientific approach to describing and classifying the insects. As a result, Rösel is regarded as one of the fathers of German entomology.

Tab. XIII

2.

In 1753, the same year in which he added "von Rosenhof" to his name, he published the first part of his second major work, *Historia naturalis ranarum nostratium*, which was completed in 1758. The quality of the work, particularly its illustrations, makes it one of the most beautiful works devoted to these amphibians. The text is printed in two columns, one in German and the other in Latin, and describes the natural history of all German frogs and toads in great detail. Despite the importance of the text, of far more interest are the twenty-four folio plates produced by copper engravings. They show, for example, the habitats, reproductive behavior, anatomical preparations, individual organs, skeletons, and various stages of larval development. All the illustrations demonstrate high artistic value in the detail and design, and in the beautiful work of the hand coloring. Each of the plates is presented twice: once in black and white with the scientific figure labels corresponding with the textual descriptions, and again colored, without the figure labels.

The enormous amount of detailed, *accurate* information in this volume compares strikingly with other volumes of this kind written in the same general time period. For instance, Mark Catesby's 1754 volume *The natural history of Caroline, Florida, and the Bahama Islands* illustrates amphibians in ways that are unrealistic and frequently barely identifiable. Albert Seba's *Locupletissimi rerum naturalium thesauri accurata descriptio* (1734) is typical of the time for illustrating hearsay or fictional organisms along with accurate depictions of those that did exist. Even the iconic 1758 catalog of life by Carl Linnaeus, *Systema naturae*, is spare, containing almost no useful information beyond minimalist statements of differentia. Rösel's volume on German frogs represents in a very real sense the beginning of accurate life-history observation in amphibians.

Several frogs illustrated by Rösel von Rosenhof became types—the name-bearing individuals that allow attachment to living populations of species names in the formal system of scientific nomenclature—of several German frog species. Examples include *Bufo calamita* (Laurenti, 1768) now *Epidalea calamita* based on the animals on plate 24 in *Historia naturalis ranarum nostratium*; *Bufo fuscus* (Laurenti, 1768) now *Pelobates fuscus* based on animals figured in plates 17 and 18; and *Rana esculenta* (Linnaeus, 1758) now *Pelophylax* kl. *esculentus* based on animals figured on plates 13, 14, and the frontispiece.

Rösel von Rosenhof started another volume on lizards and salamanders—considered to be closely related at the time—but died unexpectedly, apparently of a stroke, on March 27, 1759, before he was able to complete it.

2. The green frog (*Pelophylax lessonae*) in profile and in the process of amplexus, egg deposition, and fertilization.

3. & 4. To provide a key to features on the colored plates, uncolored "key" plates were added, whose figures were numbered and specific features labeled with letters referenced in the text. While nearly identical, two unique plates had to be engraved to accomplish this elaborate solution. These plates depict the dissection, viscera, and skeleton of the spadefoot, *Pelobates fuscus*.

5. Green frog (*Pelophylax* kl. *esculentus*) dissection showing egg masses, liver, lungs, heart, and stomach. Below, ovaries, oviducts, and associated fat bodies, as well as a skeleton drawn in the position of the dissected frog, are shown.

6. The development of the spadefoot, *Pelobates fuscus*, from recently emerged larva to froglet.

Darrel Frost is a curator in the Herpetology Department in the Division of Vertebrate Zoology at the American Museum of Natural History.

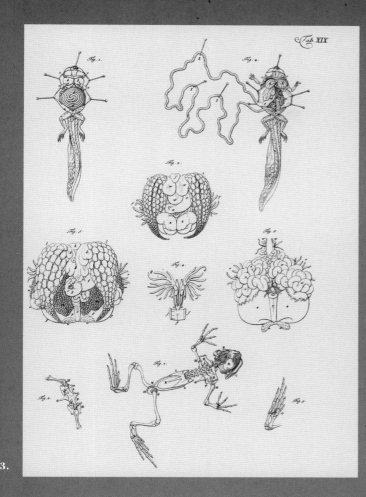

Tab. XIX

3.

Tab. XIX

4.

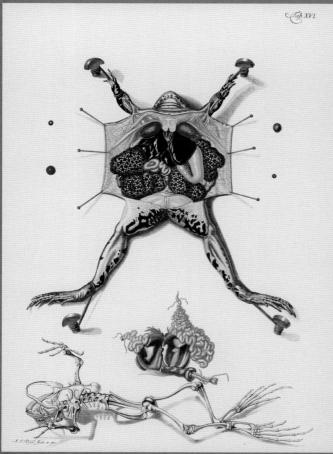

Tab. XVI

5.

Tab. XVIII

6.

Marmoris fiſſilis fodina
prope Solenhofen in
Marchionatu Onoldino.

Knorr's Fossil Treasures from Solnhofen

NEIL H. LANDMAN

Author
Georg Wolfgang Knorr
(1705–1761)

Title
Recueil de monumens des catastrophes que le globe terrestre a éssuiées, contenant des pétrifications dessinées, gravées et enluminées d'après les originaux, commencé par feu mr. George Wolfgang Knorr, et continué par ses Héritiers avec l'histoire naturelle de ces corps par mr. Jean Ernest Emanuel Walch

(Collections of remains from the catastrophes that earth has sustained, containing petrifications drawn, engraved, and illuminated from the originals, begun by the late Mr. George Wolfgang Knorr and continued by his heirs, with a natural history commentary by Mr. Jean Ernest Emanuel Walch)

Imprint
Nuremberg: [s.n.]
1768–1778

1. Hand-colored frontispiece engraving of one of the Solnhofen limestone quarries. Note the eighteenth-century costumes of the miners and the figure of the artist set in the lower right part of the frame—perhaps a self-portrait of Knorr himself.

The artist and natural scientist Georg Wolfgang Knorr was born in Nuremberg, Germany, in 1705. The library at the American Museum of Natural History owns a copy of his geological magnum opus, *Recueil de monumens des catastrophes que le globe terrestre a éssuiées, contenant des pétrifications dessinées, gravées et enluminées d'après les originaux*. This multivolume work is an expanded version of his earlier work in his native German, *Sammlung von merckwürdigkeiten der natur und alterthümern des erdbodens* (*Collections of natural wonders and antiquities of the Earth's crust*). The greatly expanded French edition contains 274 plates in several colors of ink and hand washed in watercolors, and features minerals, plants, and fossils of both vertebrates and invertebrates. The scientific text was written by Jean Ernest Emanuel Walch, who was responsible for completing the work after Knorr's death, culminating in four volumes, first published in German in 1755 and reprinted in French and Dutch editions.

Knorr's birthplace was close to some of the most fossiliferous sites in Europe, and these fossils are showcased in his color plates. In particular, he devotes plates to fossil cephalopods, mostly ammonites from the Mesozoic era, which began around 250 million years ago. During this time, large parts of Europe were covered by shallow seas inhabited by many kinds of animals that left a rich fossil record in the sedimentary rocks of the area.

Ammonites belong to the group Cephalopoda, one of the classes of Mollusca. Modern cephalopods include the pearly nautilus, squid, cuttlefish, and octopus. Like the pearly nautilus—but unlike squid—their extinct relatives the ammonites were equipped with a hard external shell composed of calcium carbonate. Commonly, the shells were coiled in a spiral shape and ornamented with elongated ridges radiating out from the center. Ammonite shells may have originally been brightly colored, like many modern mollusks, but the original colors are almost never preserved. Instead, the colors of most ammonite specimens, like the ones illustrated by Knorr, simply reflect the vagaries of fossilization. For example, the black color of some ammonite specimens matches the color of the muddy sediments, now rock, in which the ammonites were buried.

One of the most distinctive features of ammonites is that the shell is subdivided into a series of chambers of progressively increasing sizes, which are beautifully shown in many of the illustrations by Knorr (see figure 2). The chambers are separated by partitions, technically known as septa. During the lifetime of an ammonite, these chambers were filled with air, providing buoyancy for the animal to swim above the sea bottom, much like the modern nautilus. In some species, the septa became very convoluted, producing intricate patterns (sutures) where the septa attached to the inside surface of the shell wall (see figure 3). These intricate patterns are used by specialists to classify ammonite species into different families.

Knorr was not only a scientist but also a gifted artist. He included in his work a detailed illustration of one of the most famous fossiliferous sites in Germany, the Solnhofen quarry near Nuremberg, located in the southern Franconian Alb. The Solnhofen rock is a yellowish-white limestone dating from the Jurassic period (approximately 205 to 145 million years ago), which was originally deposited in a lagoon bordering the sea. The large engraving, covering a two-folio-page spread frontispiece, is beautifully hand colored and provides some marvelous detail of an eighteenth-century mining operation (see figure 1).

This and similar quarries in the region have been exploited for thousands of years. The rock has long been used for building stones because of its facility of breaking along horizontal planes, which is conveyed by its German name *Plattenkalk*, meaning "platy limestone." As an indication of its longstanding appeal, Solnhofen limestone has been found in Roman ruins in Germany, where it was used for lining baths. More recently, it has been used for pavement stones and roofing tiles in local houses.

Knorr, with his interest in natural history, would have been attracted to the Solnhofen quarries because of their famous fossils. Such fossils mostly consist of marine organisms, including fish, crinoids, ammonites, crustaceans (see figure 5), jellyfish, and squid. In the case of ammonites, although the original shell is never preserved, a large percentage of them still retain the jaws of the animal in the body chamber. In addition to marine organisms, the Solnhofen quarry contains terrestrial fossils—most famous of all, the *Archaeoptyrx*. The first specimen of this animal was discovered in the mid-nineteenth century, nearly one hundred years after Knorr's publication. This animal was long viewed as the missing link between birds and reptiles, but has now been joined by several feathered dinosaurs from China, making the story much more complicated. Nevertheless, *Archaeoptyrx* remains one of the most iconographic fossils in paleontology. Imagine how excited Knorr would have been by its discovery in the very quarries he visited and illustrated in his book!

6.

2. The specimen on the bottom is an ammonite cut in half showing the hollow chambers that would have been filled with air during the animal's life.

3. All of these specimens are parts of ammonites. The long, curved specimen exhibits the complex suture patterns used to identify different ammonite species.

4. Dendrites from the Solnhofen limestone quarry, giving the impression of a forested landscape.

5. Decapod crustaceans from the Solnhofen limestone quarries. The one in the middle is set off by a dendrite—a black mineral that forms a fern-like pattern.

6. An engraved portrait of George Wolfgang Knorr from *Recueil de monumens des catastrophes*.

Neil H. Landman is a curator in the Division of Paleontology at the American Museum of Natural History.

2.

Fig. 1-5. Ex Museo dectiss. Andreæ, pharmacop. Hannoverani. Fig. 6. Ex Museo
Excell. ac experientiss. D. Güntheri, Sereniss. Ducis Saxo-Coburg. medici
aulici et practici civitatis Cahlensis.

J. A. Fleninger sc. 230.

3.

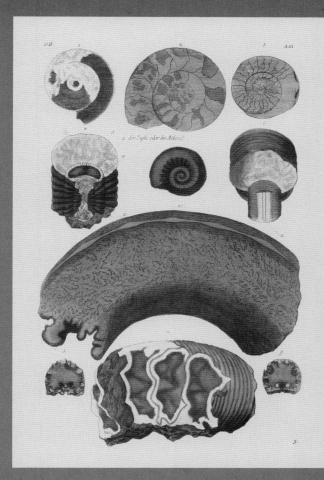

4.

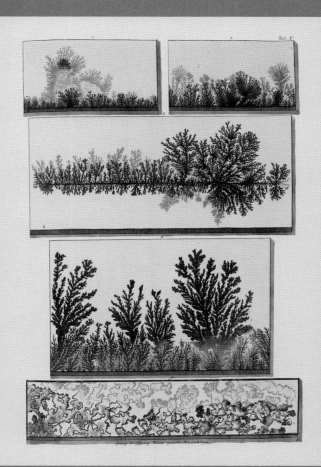

5.

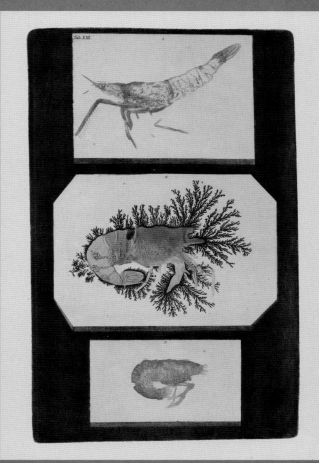

Neues Systematisches Conchylien Cabinet

geordnet und beschrieben

von

Fried: Heinrich Wilhelm Martini

der Arzneygelahrtheit Doktor und Prakticus

in Berlin.

Nürnberg

bey Gabriel Nikolaus Raspe.

Martini and Chemnitz's Iconographic Encyclopedia of Mollusks

LOUISE M. CROWLEY

Author
Friedrich Heinrich Wilhelm
Martini (1729–1778) and
Johann Hieronymus Chemnitz
(1730–1800)

Title
*Neues systematisches
conchylien-cabinet*

(New systematic shell-cabinet)

Imprint
Nürnberg: Nicolaus Raspe,
1769–1829

1. Hand-colored, copper engraved frontispiece of Volume 1 of *Neues systematisches conchylien-cabinet*, printed in 1769. This title page (indicating Martini and Raspe as author and publisher, respectively) depicts a fantastical scene of Neptune being hoisted by mermaids, with horses pulling a "shelled" chariot behind.

The *Neues systematisches conchylien-cabinet* (*New systematic shell-cabinet*) is one of the largest iconographies of shells and is one of the most famous works in malacology (the study of mollusks). This monographic series is one of the first of its kind, with more than 4,000 drawings of shells—many illustrated and described for the first time—indicating different aspects of a great number of molluscan species. The work was incredibly comprehensive for its time, with all of the known molluscan classes represented. The detail and clarity of descriptions of these shells were, for that time, beyond compare. In addition to providing detailed diagnoses of each mollusk shell, the authors referenced earlier works, including most notably those of Carl Linnaeus, Georg Wolfgang Knorr, Georg Eberhard Rumphius, and Albert Seba. Also striking is the intricate quality of the finely engraved, hand-colored plates. Moreover, the vignettes, which are dispersed throughout the text, either demonstrate the organisms in animated, life-like poses or capture internal details of the shells. To this day, the colors appear vivid, but true to form—Martini had the specimens illustrated in a realistic manner, not so that they would be simply pleasing to the eye.

The series was a huge undertaking initiated by the Berlin physician Friedrich Heinrich Wilhelm Martini. Born in Ohrdruf, a small town in the district of Gotha, in 1729, Martini initially studied theology, but soon turned to medicine. He held a great passion and love for all things related to the natural sciences, and worked tirelessly to disseminate scientific knowledge to the public. To this end, he founded several magazines—including *Das Berlinische Magazin* (*The Berlin Magazine*) and *Mannigfaltigkeiten* (*Manifolds*)—and translated many of the works of the great French naturalist Georges-Louis Leclerc Buffon into German.

Martini took enormous pleasure from the study of shells, deeming a clean and well-organized cabinet of shells to be lustful and tempting to the eye. Prior to the publication of the first volume in 1769, he devoted eight years to the preparation of this work, claiming little time for anything else. Studying specimens from his own collection and those housed at the Royal Academy of Sciences and Fine Art, Martini intended to describe and illustrate every known, as well as previously unknown, mollusk. The shells were not arranged systematically in a taxonomic sense, but were, however, arranged according to outward similarities, working from the more simple to the complex. Martini did not live to fulfill his aspiration, dying two years after the publication of the third volume.

Following his death, the task of continuing this work fell to Johann Hieronymus Chemnitz. Known as the "Danish preacher," Chemnitz was born in Magdeburg, Germany, in 1730. He was a clergyman to garrison troops in Vienna, Elsinore, and eventually Copenhagen. In addition to his pastoral duties, Chemnitz was a keen collector of shells and published a small number of contributions concerning conchology. He was a member of the Natural History Society, Berlin, a society that Martini founded.

Chemnitz took up his leadership role in earnest and published the fourth volume of *Neues systematisches conchylien-cabinet* in 1780. By the time of his death in Copenhagen in 1800, he had published eight more volumes and had a ninth in development. The majority of shells featured in Chemnitz's volumes came from his own extensive collection, as well as from that of Lorenz Spengler, a turner—a craftsman who turned and shaped wood on a lathe—to the Danish Royal Court. Spengler was a close friend of Chemnitz, and many of his featured shells can be found today in the Zoological Museum of the University of Copenhagen. Chemnitz also featured shells in collections of European royalty, including those of King Frederic V of Denmark and Maria Theresia, Empress of Austria, among others.

The importance of this work as a reference source for taxonomists is marred by the fact that neither Martini nor Chemnitz employed the binomial system for naming new species within the first eleven volumes. Binomial nomenclature is a formal system of naming species introduced by Linnaeus in 1758. Within this system, each organism is denoted by a name that consists of a genus name, to which the individual belongs, and a species name. This system is still in use today, but because it was not employed in this work, all the new descriptions of species are considered invalid. Why the authors chose not to use this system of naming is unclear, as both authors figure many Linnaean specimens in the volumes. There is, however, utility in this work, as a single source of reference for a great number of molluscan species. Moreover, Linnaeus, Johann Friedrich Gmelin, and Jean-Baptiste Lamarck often referenced Martini figures in their publication of new descriptions.

This encyclopedic work was continued by Heinrich Küster, who began editing a much larger edition entitled *Systematishces conchylien-cabinet* in 1837. This work was subsequently continued by others at intervals up until 1920.

2. Printed in red ink and signed by A. F. Kappe (one of the primary illustrators of the earlier volumes). One of many engraved headpieces, or illustrations, this illustration denotes the internal shell structure of the chambered nautilus, *Nautilus pompilius* (Linnaeus, 1758).

3. A copper-engraved print of *Triton variegatum* (currently classified as *Charonia variegata*), with five different aspects illustrated. Originally described by Lamarck (1816).

4. This plate, entitled "Mussels with Notched Hinges," shows arcoid bivalves originally described by Linnaeus and Lamarck.

5. A copper-engraved print of *Voluta magnifica* (Gebauer, 1802), the magnificent volute (currently classified as *Cymbiola magnifica*). The tabs on the side of the volume (seen in Volumes 1–11) highlight that the body text and plates were bound separately.

Louise M. Crowley is a postdoctoral fellow in the Division of Invertebrate Zoology at the American Museum of Natural History.

„ lasten sie ihre Kammern vom Wasser und bringen Luft hinein. Nun stei-
„ gen sie mit aufwärts gerichtetem Kiel in die Höhe, wenden sich und stellen
„ da ihre Fahrt an.

Auf dem Grund bringen sie die meiste Zeit zu, und gerathen daselbst bis-
weilen in die Fischkörbe, wodurch man das Schiff mit dem Steuermann zu-
gleich erhalten kann. Die geringe Bevestigung dieser wehrlosen Thiere an ih-
ren Schaalen und der Mangel eines Deckels, läßt sie leicht den Krabben,
Seehunden und Krokodillen zum Raub werden.

Ihr Fleisch ist härter und schwerer zu verdauen, als am vorigen Kuttel-
fisch, doch wird es bey den Indianern, wie andere Seethiere, zu einer nähr-
haften Speise gebraucht.

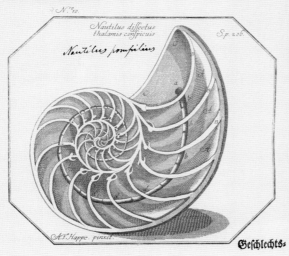

Geschlechts-

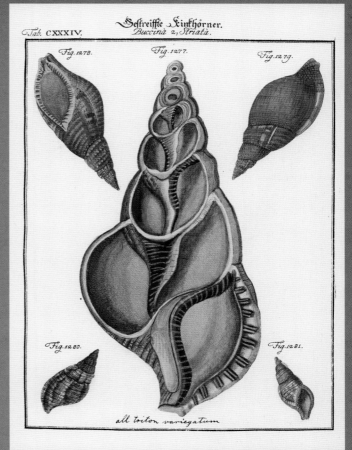

Tab. CXXXIV.

Gestreiffte Kinkhörner.
Buccina 2, Striata.

Fig. 1278. Fig. 1277. Fig. 1279.

Fig. 1280. Fig. 1281.

all triton variegatum

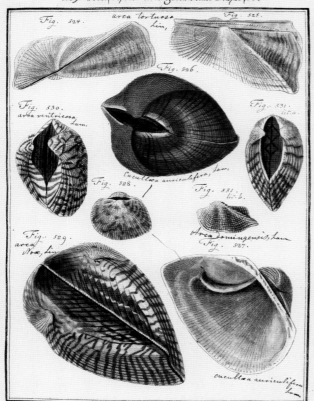

10) Muscheln mit gekerbtem Schlosse.

Fig. 524. arca tortuosa Lin, Fig. 525.

Fig. 526.

Fig. 530. arca ventricosa Lam. Fig. 531. lita.

Cucullaea auriculifera, Lam.

Fig. 528. Fig. 531. li. b.

Area domingensis, Lam.

Fig. 529. arca Noa, Lin Fig. 527.

cucullaea auriculifera Lam

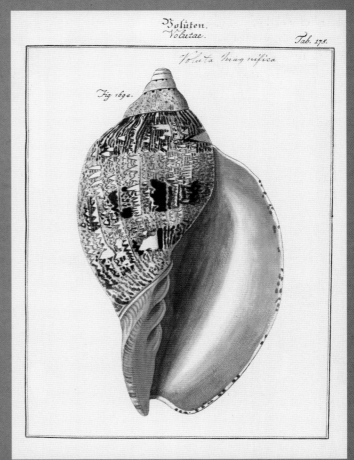

Tab. 178.

Voluten.
Volutae.

Voluta Magnifica

Fig. 1694.

2.

3.

4.

5.

Tab XII
LIBELLULÆ, Wings expanded

fig 1

b

4

a

2

3

Moses Harris: Naturalist and Artist

DAVID GRIMALDI

Author
Moses Harris
(1731–1785)

Title
*The Aurelian, or
natural history of
English insects . . .*

Imprint
London: Printed for the
author, 1766, and with great
additions for J. Robson, 1778

Title
*An exposition of English
insects . . .*

Imprint
London: Printed for the
author, 1776

Title
*Exposition of English
insects . . .*

Imprint
London: Sold by Mr. White &
Mr. Robson, 1782

1. From *Exposition*, 1782.
Two adult dragonflies with a
nymphal dragonfly.

oses Harris was an eighteenth-century naturalist and artist whose work focused on British insects, and he is often regarded as the first British entomologist. His career was launched with the 1766 publication of *The Aurelian, or natural history of English insects*, a folio volume on the life histories of principally the Lepidoptera. The book discusses and illustrates methods for collecting and preserving insects, but the most impressive aspect of the work is the elaborate depiction of moths and butterflies, complete with their caterpillars feeding on native host plants—sometimes rendered even with their eggs, fecal pellets, and the tiny parasitoid wasps that prey on their caterpillars. Harris was a keenly observant naturalist, not only in sorting out the different species of moths and butterflies, but in studying their life histories, as well.

At the time, the medium of choice for illustrations was hand-painted copper plate engravings and etchings, which took great time, skill, and expense. To pay for the work, Harris dedicated most plates of *The Aurelian* to wealthy sponsors—depicting the family crests of earls, dukes, barons, and other nobility on each plate. The text was in both English and French, the latter the language of aristocracy at the time. One plate was dedicated to the Swedish scientist Carl Linnaeus, founder of the modern system of naming species, while another was dedicated to one Dru Drury (1725–1803), Harris's "benefactor." Drury was a silversmith turned entomologist who had built a personal collection of some 11,000 insect specimens, among the largest of its time. Drury was so impressed by *The Aurelian* that he commissioned Harris to illustrate his own three-volume *Illustrations of natural history* (1770–1782), which depicted more than 240 exotic species of insects, including the first published image of the African goliath beetle.

It was standard for authors in the eighteenth and nineteenth centuries to commission artists to illustrate their work. What makes Harris unique is that he expertly illustrated his own work. Indeed, Harris was fastidious in his portrayal of the myriad colors and iridescence of butterfly wings and beetle elytra (wings), using an easily replicated system of mixing pigments and naming colors. His color system started with the three primary colors—red, yellow, and blue—positioned at the center of a circular layout, with various hues and combinations arranged concentrically. It was the first modern "color wheel." As such, it is commonly referred to as the Harris color wheel.

The first published appearance of Harris's color wheel is in a very rare, obscure, and slim work by Harris, *An exposition of English insects* (1776). Compared to *The Aurelian*, the proportions of *An exposition of English insects*—at under a foot tall—make it a veritable field guide. It contains just ten plates, each with multiple species and devoid of host plants and other embellishments. These ten plates, and his color wheel, were reprinted in Harris's later, much larger, and better-known work, *Exposition of English insects* (1782). While Lepidoptera and Coleoptera were very popular among naturalists of the time, Harris's work represented a significant departure by including other orders, such as Odonata (dragonflies and damselflies), Hemiptera (true bugs), various wasps (including bees), and Diptera (true flies). In fact, three of the ten plates in *An exposition of English insects*, surprisingly, are of flies. As a dipterist myself, such early fascination with the diversity of flies is, of course, appreciated, particularly since mosquitoes, horseflies, and other blood-feeding flies have maligned the reputations of all Diptera as pests. In fact, many of the approximately 150,000 species of flies either have no direct effect on humans, or else they play extremely beneficial ecological roles, such as pollination. In both versions of Harris's *Exposition of English insects*, flower flies (of the family Syrphidae) are a favorite, as they still are among many British amateur naturalists. What is so impressive about Harris's illustrations are the vivid colors and the anatomical accuracy. For small insects like flies, the wing veins, bristles, and color patterns on the bodies are rendered with surprising accuracy. The flies are depicted in natural poses and cast shadows, as if they had just alighted on the page.

2. From *The Aurelian*, 1766. Illustrated are the life cycles of several moths, primarily hawk moths of the family Sphingidae, including their eggs, caterpillars, host plants, and pupae, and even methods for spreading wings of specimens.

3. From *An Exposition*, 1776. Flower, or hover, flies of the family Syrphidae. Many species resemble and mimic bees and wasps.

4. From *The Aurelian*, 1766. Adult, caterpillar, and pupa of the death's head hawk moth, *Acherontia atropos*. Adults will steal honey from beehives and squeak when disturbed.

5. Color wheel from *Exposition*, 1782. A hand-painted, early version of the Harris color wheel (the modern color wheel).

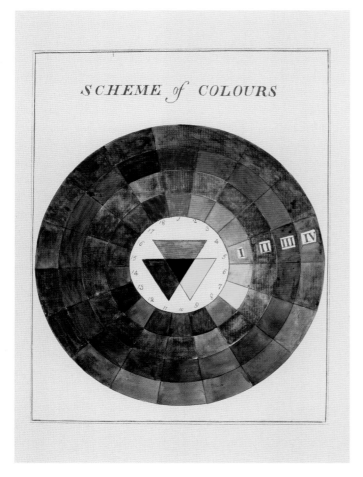

5.

***David Grimaldi** is a curator in the Entomology Department in the Division of Invertebrate Zoology at the American Museum of Natural History.*

2.

PL. XX.

To Her Grace the [coat of arms] Dutchefs of Richmond.
This Plate is humbly Dedicated by her Graces most Oblig.d & Obed.t Hum.le Serv.t
Moses Harris.

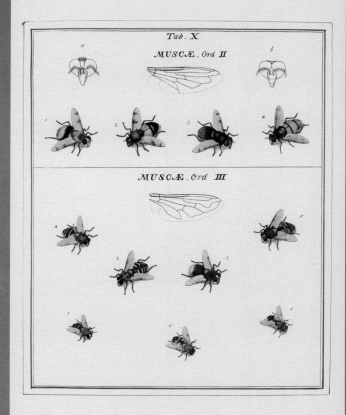

3.

Tab. X

MUSCÆ. Ord II

MUSCÆ. Ord III

To my Ingenous Friend and Benefactor M.r Dru Drury
This Plate is moft Humbly Dedicated by his Obliged Servant Mofes Harris

4.

SOCIETATI REGIÆ LONDINI
GULIELMUS HAMILTON
BALN·ORD·EQUES·
D·D·D·
CIↃIↃCCLXXIX·

Observing Vesuvius with Sir William Hamilton

JAMES WEBSTER

Author
William Hamilton
(1731–1803), illustrated by
Pietro Fabris (1740–1792)

Title
*Campi Phlegraei:
observations on the
volcanoes of the Two Sicilies*

Imprint
Naples: [s.n.] 1776

1. The frontispiece from Hamilton's 1779 supplement to *Campi Phlegraei* depicts several eruptions of Vesuvius in the years 1777 to 1779. Like all the illustrations in *Campi Phlegraei*, the fine-lined engraving and artful coloring give the impression that each illustration is an original painting.

A diplomat by profession, Sir William Hamilton was also an accomplished scholar, archeologist, and natural historian. He developed keen skills in observing volcanic rocks and landforms that led him to pioneer field investigations of Italy's largest volcanoes. Hamilton served as ambassador to the court of Naples and, from 1764 to 1800, as the envoy extraordinary from the United Kingdom to the Two Sicilies. During his posting in Italy, he mounted sixty-eight expeditions on the hazardous slopes of Mount Somma-Vesuvius, and he was often found on the volcano observing it while it was erupting. Based on his expeditions, rocks collected in the field, and extensive telescope-based scrutiny of Somma-Vesuvius, Hamilton wrote exacting descriptions of his scientific observations. He combined his written accounts with beautiful geologic illustrations of individual rock specimens, rock outcrops, volcanic craters, and the occasional eruption, and published them as *Campi Phlegraei: observations on the volcanoes of the Two Sicilies* in 1776.

Hamilton conducted his scientific work in an age and location that were active, both culturally and geologically. During the mid- to late-eighteenth century, the archeological excavations of Pompeii and Herculaneum, which were buried by the A.D. 79 Somma-Vesuvius eruption, were made. Artifacts recovered from these ancient cities were of great interest to Hamilton. Also, there was no shared technical language at that time for the scientists who studied volcanoes, because the science of volcanology was only just being developed. Moreover, Somma-Vesuvius was highly active. It erupted three times during Hamilton's posting in Naples, and these events allowed him to observe, collect samples, and describe the diverse volcanic events associated with the eruptions. Of note in this regard, Hamilton made the first quantitative measurements and sketches of the changing surface morphology of Somma-Vesuvius during the 1776 eruption.

Historically, Hamilton's scientific achievements are truly profound given that he had no formal scientific training and that—prior to his work—the early interpretations of volcanic activities were often colored by religious or ethereal connotations. Independently, Hamilton developed his own approach for the methodological characterization of volcanoes and their rare pyrotechnic-eruptive events.

This folio edition of Hamilton's descriptive work was written originally as scholarly letters that were read at meetings of the Royal Society of London. Later, the letters were supported by a new map that included geologic features of the Bay of Naples region and fifty-four hand-colored plates with "exhilarating effect" that were together published as *Campi Phlegraei*. Copies were provided to fellows of the Royal Society and sold to others in English and French, and the resulting work was quite costly for the time.

2.

The images were created by Neapolitan artist Pietro Fabris, who accompanied Hamilton on his geological wanderings. Under Hamilton's scrutiny, Fabris made the original drawings, which were later colored and detailed as gouache works. The printing process involved copper engraving followed by hand coloring, and the original engravings were made faint so that after filling in the outlines with gouache paint, the finished works appear much like original paintings. This set of books was purchased by the American Museum of Natural History's library from a London dealer in 1919.

Based on his extensive observations, writings, and supporting field images, Hamilton is still acknowledged as the most reliable source of information on the late-eighteenth-century eruptions of Vesuvius. Years later, Charles Lyell—author of *Principles of Geology*, the preeminent geologic text of its time—used *Campi Phlegraei* as the reference for Vesuvius and its eruptive features and activities. Although modern volcanologists employ extremely sophisticated observational and analytical techniques to study the Earth, the basic understanding of volcanology is still knowing which rocks and landforms to focus on and how to interpret their origins—in other words, the skills that Hamilton helped to develop and share as the science of volcanology came into its own.

2. These landscape plates display Hamilton, characteristically attired in his red field coat, surveying the volcanic terrains around Naples. In one striking night image, Somma-Vesuvius is in full eruption, and Hamilton has escorted the Sicilian majesties to observe the vast flows of lava and billowing clouds of volcanic gases in 1771.

3. Eruptions of any single volcano are typically rare in a human lifetime, so the day-to-day work of volcanologists is based on discerning and reading narratives in rocks either recently or long-since erupted. Following this approach, Hamilton shares his observations and interpretations with colleagues at the dormant and extinct volcanic cones and craters of *Campi Phlegraei* in this plate.

4. Hamilton walks through craggy, upthrusted volcanic spires of the older Monte Somma crater with the younger volcanic cone of Vesuvius steaming away in the background. To Hamilton, these features were evidence that volcanoes are not simply destructive but that "mountains are produced by volcanoes."

5. Sketches of volcanic rock samples are shown, and mineral crystals are visible on rock surfaces and in the open volcanic pockets of the rocks. A mysterious jeweled pin is included with these natural specimens.

James Webster is a curator in the Earth and Planetary Science Department in the Division of Physical Sciences at the American Museum of Natural History.

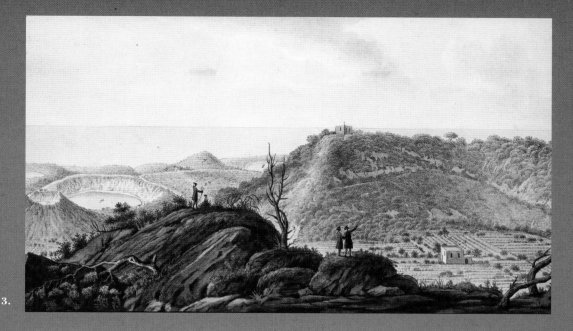

3.

4.

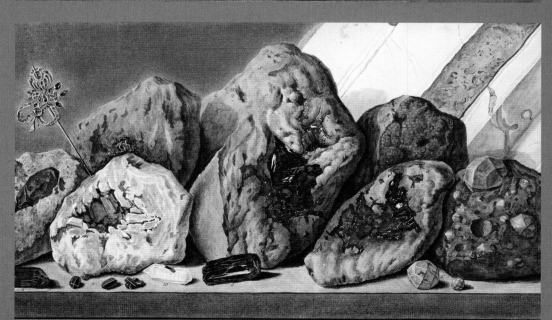

5.

The Volumes of Cramer and Stoll:
A Timeless Contribution to the Science
of Butterflies and Moths

JAMES S. MILLER

Author
Pieter Cramer (1721–1776)

Title
*De uitlandsche kapellen
voorkomende in de drie
waereld-deelen Asia, Africa
en America*

*(Exotic lepidoptera from three
regions of the world, Asia,
Africa and America)*

Imprint
Amsterlam: Chez S. J.
Baalde, 1779–1782

Pieter Cramer, born in Amsterdam in 1721, was a wealthy linen and wool merchant who had an avid interest in natural history. Lepidoptera—the scientific term for butterflies and moths—were his passion. Cramer himself never collected in the field, but he assembled a large Lepidoptera collection through purchase and trade. Most of his specimens came from countries that the Dutch had colonized—Suriname, Sri Lanka (then Ceylon), and Indonesia (then the Dutch East Indies)—but his collection also included material from North America, Africa, and Asia.

Cramer decided to hire the little-known Amsterdam artist Gerrit Wartenaar to create a permanent record of his collection. The high quality and detail in the resulting hand-colored plates were such that Cramer was encouraged to publish them. In his *De uitlandsche kapellen* (*Exotic lepidoptera*), each moth and butterfly illustration was accompanied by a brief diagnosis, written by Cramer, of the antennal shape and wing pattern for that particular species. All told, four hundred plates—figuring 1,658 moth and butterfly species—were published between the years 1775 and 1782. The plates and their accompanying text were published in thirty-four parts, offered to a list of subscribers, with one issue being sent out every three months. The complete work was compiled into four volumes.

Although these remarkable books are invariably attributed to Pieter Cramer, additional people were instrumental in seeing the project to fruition. When Cramer died of a fever in 1776 at the age of 55, only the first volume of *De uitlandsche kapellen* had been published. Volume 2 was evidently ready for immediate publication because it appeared in 1777, soon after Cramer's death. The remaining parts were nearly complete. Cramer had stipulated in his will that the plates were to go to his nephew and business partner, Anthony Wellemzoon van Rensselaar, for future publication. Van Rensselaar enlisted the help of Caspar Stoll, who had been involved with the production of the first volume. Stoll exerted considerable influence on subsequent volumes and wrote the text for most of Volume 4, from page 29 onward. Between the years 1787 and 1790, Stoll published an important supplement to the work, comprising forty-two plates of 250 additional Lepidoptera, including illustrations of the larvae and pupae of many rare species from Suriname.

Several things make *De uitlandsche kapellen* unique. First, not only is each moth and butterfly shown life-size, but also the upper *and* lower wing surfaces are figured. This imparts high scientific value to the illustrations; for many Lepidoptera, the pattern on the lower wing's surface—though less gaudy—provides better features for recognition than that on the upper surface. Second, this was the first treatise on Lepidoptera to use the then newly developed classification system of Carl Linnaeus.

1. Cramer and Stoll treated Lepidoptera from the far reaches of the earth. A pierid butterfly, *Hebomoia leucippe* (A–C), from Ambon Island, Indonesia, dominates the illustration. The plate also shows an obscure Prominent Moth, *Rosema deolis* (F), from Suriname.

Accordingly, each butterfly and moth species was assigned to a genus following the rules of binomial nomenclature that is still employed today. Cramer and Stoll were pioneers, laying the groundwork for future generations of lepidopterists. Cramer and Stoll followed Linnaeus in dividing all Lepidoptera into only three genera, depending on their flight habits: Butterflies ("Papillons Diurnes") were placed in a single genus, *Papilio*. Today the 18,000 butterfly species are assigned to six families comprising 1,500 genera. Their second genus was *Sphinx* ("Papillons du Soir"); modern classifications regard sphinx moths to be a family of 1,200 species placed in more than two hundred genera. Their final genus, *Phalaenae* ("Papillons Nocturnes"), contained all the remaining moths. Moths are currently divided into 117 families comprising tens of thousands of genera and an estimated 230,000 named species.

There is a third, fundamentally unique aspect of these books. In their accounts of the figured moths and butterflies, Cramer and Stoll acknowledged those species that had already been given a valid scientific name. However, many of the Lepidoptera shown in *De uitlandsche kapellen* were new to science. In these cases, Cramer and Stoll assigned a name, but their diagnoses and figures take on special significance because they became the formal description for that species. These volumes thus contain hundreds of what are called "original descriptions"—the unique account that first establishes the scientific name for any animal or plant species.

As a lepidopterist, I refer to *De uitlandsche kapellen* on a regular basis. For example, in my research on Prominent Moths (family Notodontidae), it was essential that I understand the correct identity of a species currently called *Erbessa priverna*, from northern South America. The original description of *priverna* comprises Cramer's text and figure, published as part of Volume 2 in 1777 (see figure 5). By referring to those, I was able to resolve the identity of that moth species. Thus, *De uitlandsche kapellen* not only is a rare work containing beautiful illustrations of Lepidoptera and an essential reference for scientists working today, but also will remain invaluable for future generations to come.

2.

2. The frontispiece pays tribute to two of Cramer's inspirations whose books lie on top of the stone monument: Linnaeus, the Swedish botanist-zoologist whose work laid the foundations for biological classification, and Merian, an artist-naturalist who spent eighteen years documenting the plants and insects of Suriname.

3. Three butterflies are shown: *Junonia orithya* (C, D) occurring from Africa to Australia; *Polygonia interrogationis* (E, F) from North America; and *Morpho menelaus* (A, B) from South America. Cramer noted that *menelaus* was also figured in books by two of his mentors, Linnaeus and Merian.

4. The Cramer/Stoll volumes showcase moths as well as butterflies. This plate illustrates five tropical Hawk Moths (A–F; family Sphingidae), including *Cocytius antaeus* (A), the only insect with a tongue long enough to pollinate the rare ghost orchid.

5. This plate features two swallowtail butterflies, *Papilio memnon* (A) and *Papilio cresphontes* (B), as well as the Rattlebox Moth, *Utetheisa ornatrix* (C, D, F). *Erbessa priverna* (E) is a rare South American Prominent Moth.

6. In addition to a small satyr butterfly, *Chloreuptychia herseis* (C, D), this plate figures one of the world's most famous butterflies, *Troides hypolitus* (A, B)—or Rippon's Birdwing—from the Moluccas and Sulawesi.

James S. Miller is a research associate in the Entomology Department in the Division of Invertebrate Zoology at the American Museum of Natural History.

3.

4.

5.

6.

TRIGLA VOLITANS.
Der fliegende Seehahn.
L'Arondel de Mer.
The Flying-Fish.

...ns-Agenten Herrn v. Cobres in Augsburg.

351.

J. F. Hennig sc.

Bloch's Remarkable Fishes

MELANIE L. J. STIASSNY

Author
Marcus Elieser Bloch
(1723–1799)

Title
*Allgemeine Naturgeschichte
der Fische*

*(General natural history
of fishes)*

Imprint
Berlin: Auf Kosten der
Verfassers und in Commission
bei dem Buchhändler Hr.
Hess, 1782–1795

The scientific study of fishes came rather late in life to the German physician-surgeon Marcus Elieser Bloch, yet from the age of forty-seven, when he began his ichthyological studies, Bloch established himself as one of the founding fathers of the modern discipline. Publication of his magnificent *Allgemeine Naturgeschichte der Fische* (*General natural history of fishes*), a stunningly illustrated and scholarly compendium of all fishes known at that time, received universal recognition and established Bloch's place among the scientific elite of the European Enlightenment—a position of esteem he maintains to this day.

Unlike many of his contemporaries, Bloch did not come from privilege, but was born into very modest circumstances. His father was a respected but poorly paid Torah writer in the Jewish community of Ansbach, Germany. Bloch's secular schooling was minimal, and by the age of nineteen he could not read or write, neither in German nor Latin. Through much hard work under the tutelage of a Hamburg surgeon, he gained sufficient linguistic and medical knowledge to study anatomy in Berlin. As a Jew he was barred from obtaining a doctorate there, so he moved to Frankfurt to continue his medical studies. It was not until the age of forty-two that he received a license to practice as a physician in Berlin. There, he maintained a busy and apparently lucrative medical practice and published a number of influential medical papers.

Bloch married three times, and the considerable dowry of his second wife probably helped to support his studies of natural history in addition to the amassing of a much renowned cabinet of natural objects. Most of the fishes in Bloch's famous collection—some 1,400 in all—are today housed in the Natural History Museum of Humboldt University in Berlin. Because of the importance of Bloch's studies—in the *Allgemeine* alone, 267 species new to science were described—these specimens remain of inestimable scientific value and continue to this day to be examined by ichthyologists from around the globe. It is in good part, because Bloch based many of his descriptions and illustrations on actual specimens, which lend such singular importance to this groundbreaking ichthyological work (rather than relying entirely on the accounts and sketches of collectors, as had many of his predecessors).

It seems that Bloch's interest in fishes was established after he observed that certain well-known German fishes were not included in the authoritative reference works of his day, such as those of Carl Linneaus and Peter Artedi. Bloch set about compiling a comprehensive guide to all fishes of the German states. Between 1782 and 1784, he published the three-volume *Oeconomische Naturegeschichte der Fische Deutchlands*. Among the accompanying 108 large-scale, colored, copper plate engravings is a depiction of the gibel, a carp common in German waters but apparently

1. *Trigla volitans.* The flying gurnard, today included in the genus *Dactylopterus*, is found throughout the coastal waters of the Atlantic Ocean. Unlike true flying fishes, the gurnard is a bottom-dweller that uses the finger-like anterior rays of its massive pectoral fins to crawl over sand and mud and probe the substrate for food.

2.

unknown to any of his predecessors, and for which Bloch provided the first scientific description and the name *Cyprinus gibelio*. While our understanding of relationships, as reflected in their generic assignment, has changed since Bloch's day and the fish that he described as *Cyprinus gibelio* is currently placed, along with the common goldfish, in the genus *Carassius*, his species description remains valid.

Bloch extended his studies with the ambitious goal of describing all known fishes. His growing recognition as a scientific authority, his wealth, and a network of collectors and colleagues overseas provided him with many specimens. Some were dignitaries of high rank including King Friedrich II of Prussia and notables such as Sir William Hamilton—English envoy to the court of Naples—but most were missionaries and surgeons working in the far-flung corners of European empires. The result, published between 1785 and 1795, was the *Naturgeschichte der ausländischen Fische* in nine volumes with 324 color plates. Thus, it is the combined *Oeconomische Naturegeschichte der Fische Deutchlands* and *Naturgeschichte der ausländischen Fische*—bound together in twelve volumes with 432 consecutively numbered color plates—that have come to be known as Bloch's *Allgemeine Naturgeschichte der Fische*.

Fishes are notoriously difficult subjects to capture visually, and many of Bloch's illustrations not only are accurate depictions but also beautifully capture the sense of the animal in life. His spot-fin porcupinefish (*Diodon hystrix*) is accurately depicted in its inflated state, clearly displaying twenty or so spines between its snout and dorsal fin. This characteristic number of spines and some features of color pattern allow us to easily distinguish this species from a similar-looking relative, the balloonfish (*Diodon holocanthus*), which appears in the same waters. It is interesting to note that many of Bloch's original illustrations show an eye glint, indicating that each specimen was removed from its liquid preservative for examination and artistic rendering (underwater, no such glint is present). Accompanying most images is a diagrammatic cross-section through the abdomen, thereby providing a sense of the three-dimensionality and disposition of body musculature in each species—suggesting that Bloch may have dissected many of the species he described in his opus.

It is surely a testament to the enduring importance of Bloch's work that centuries after he labored on it, contemporary ichthyologists are still actively engaged in studying it. As recently as 1987, one of my own ichthyological mentors at the British Museum of Natural History, Ethelwynn Trewavas, an authority of African fishes, was able to determine, based on Bloch's meticulous drawing and description of the fish *Labrus melagaster* from Suriname, that it was, in fact, the West African cichlid *Sarotherodon melanotheron*. Apparently, Bloch often omitted locality information from his growing handwritten catalog of specimens and relied on memory to fill in data in his publications. Given the tremendous scope of this monumental work, it is not at all surprising that a few mistakes have crept in here and there; but, rather more surprising is the fact that so much of what he wrote remains valid to this day.

2. The beautiful engraved vignette on this title page depicts a naiad and cherubs cavorting with fishes.

3. *Cyprinus gibelio*. Commonly known as the Prussian carp, this fish is widespread in the freshwaters of central Europe to Siberia. The enigmatic fish is currently placed in the genus *Carassius* and possibly represents the wild form introduced to eastern Asia and subsequently domesticated into the ornamental goldfish.

4. *Diodon hystrix*. This beautifully rendered spot-fin porcupinefish is a species that occurs circumtropically in shallow-water lagoons and seaward reefs. Most individuals are solitary and nocturnal and use their beak-like teeth to eat hard-shelled sea urchins and crabs.

5. *Labrus melagaster* (far right). Bloch mistakenly described this fish as a member of the marine wrasse genus *Labrus*. His careful description and clear illustration allowed for a correct identification as a freshwater fish, the blackchin tilapia (*Sarotherodon melanotheron*), found in estuaries and coastal rivers of West Africa.

Melanie L. J. Stiassny *is the Axelrod Curator of Fishes in the Ornithology Department in the Division of Vertebrate Zoology at the American Museum of Natural History.*

3.

XII. Taf.

Natürliche Größe.

CYPRINUS GIBELIO.
Die Giebel.

4.

Taf. CXXVI.

DIODON HYSTRIX.
Der runde Stachelfisch.
Le Guara.

5.

CCXCVI.

LABRUS MALAPTERUS
Der Weichflosser.
Le Labre à nageoires molles.

LABRUS MELAGASTER
Der Schwarzbauch.
Le Mélagastre.

Fig. 2

Fig. 1

Gestochen auf Kosten S. Fürstl. Durchlaucht des regierenden Herzogs von Würtemberg.

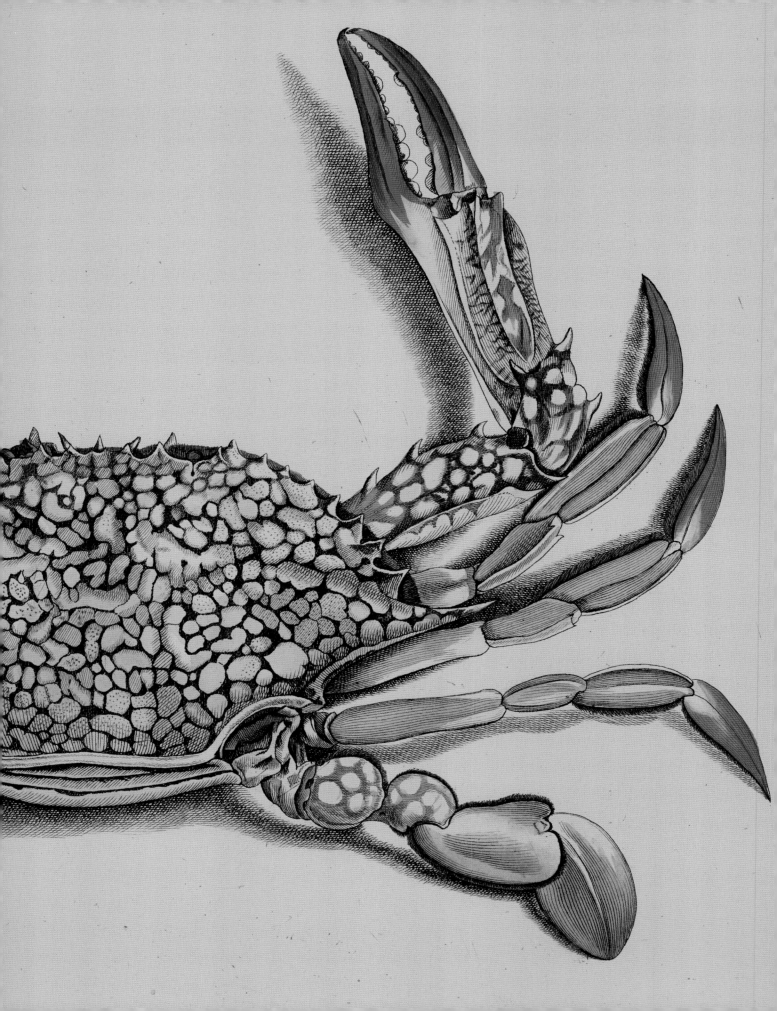

A Beautiful Harvest:
Herbst's Crabs and Crayfish

BELLA GALIL

Author
Johann Friederich Wilhelm
Herbst (1743–1807)

Title
*Versuch einer Naturgeschichte
der Krabben und Krebse
nebst einer systematischen
Beschreibung ihrer
verschieden Arten*

*(Attempt at a natural history
of crabs and crayfish,
including a systematic
description of the various
genera)*

Imprint
Zurich: Joh. Casper Fuessly,
1782–1804

Johann Friederich Wilhelm Herbst was a member of a small circle of German and English churchmen in the eighteenth and nineteenth centuries who, in addition to their pastoral duties, sought a better understanding of the workings of nature through classification. Their devotion laid the basis for the modern study of natural history. Herbst's monographs on Insecta—which at the time comprised all arthropods—are among the most beautiful and lovingly illustrated volumes ever produced.

Herbst was born in Petershagen, Minden principality, in the Kingdom of Prussia, where his father was senior priest and superintendent of the principality. Herbst followed in his father's steps and studied theology at the University of Halle. On completing his course of studies, Herbst entered the service of a distinguished local family and later joined the household of the counselor and city magistrate Weitzel in Berlin. In 1769, Herbst was ordained and received a post as a military chaplain in a Prussian infantry regiment. A year later, he returned to Berlin as chaplain of the Königlichen Cadetten Institute. In 1782, following a short foray as senior priest in Reppen, Torgau-Oschatz, Herbst assumed the position of subdeacon in St. Marien Church in Berlin, where he stayed for the next twenty-five years.

In Berlin, Herbst befriended the talented entomologist and illustrator Carl Gustav Jablonsky, who served as private secretary to the queen of Prussia. Together, Jablonsky and Herbst attempted a complete survey of the Insecta. After Jablonsky's untimely death in 1787, Herbst spent the next two decades editing and publishing the superbly illustrated work *Natursystem aller bekannten in und ausländischen Insecten, als eine Fortzetsung der von Büffonschen Naturgeschichte. Nach dem System des Ritters Carl von Linné bearbeitet* (1785–1806), which Jablonsky had begun. At the same time, Herbst undertook the study of decapod crustaceans, describing and illustrating numerous new species, some from the Mediterranean Sea and the Americas, but mostly those from the Indo-Pacific Ocean. Herbst obtained many of the specimens from his eminent contemporary J. C. Fabricius, and from duplicates sent by naturalist friends who made entire collections available to him. Herbst's crustacean collection grew so important that it was bought posthumously by Prussian King Frederick William III and donated in 1810 to the newly founded University in Berlin, where it is housed to this day.

A recent study,[1] combining morphometrics and DNA sequencing, has borne out Herbst's keen observations and faithful rendering. Herbst described and illustrated two species of swimming crabs, *Cancer cedonulli* (figure 3) and *C. reticulatus* (figure 1). Subsequent authors considered both to be identical to *C. pelagicus*, a species that had been described earlier by Linnaeus. Since only one

1. *Portunus* (*Portunus*) *reticulatus* (Herbst, 1799) (*Cancer reticulatus* Herbst, 1799). This species is restricted to the Bay of Bengal.

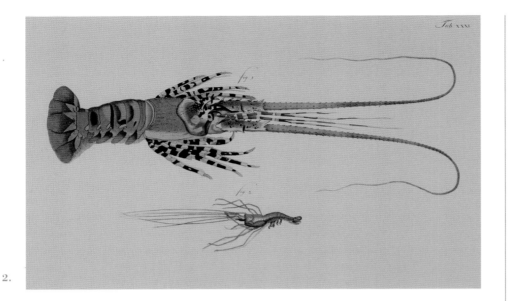

Tab. XXXI

2.

scientific name is considered to be correct at any given time and other scientific names applied to the same taxon are called synonyms, Herbst's species were considered junior synonyms of *Portunus pelagicus* (Linnaeus, 1758). However, a close examination of Herbst's illustrations shows he depicted *C. cedonulli* [syn. *Portunus pelagicus* (Linnaeus, 1758)] with the characteristic white spots on the carapace (shell) merging into broad reticulations, in particular on the posterior and branchial regions, while the carapace of *C. reticulatus* [*P. reticulatus* (Herbst, 1799)] is covered with spots, rarely merging into short bands. Herbst's unambiguous illustrations and meticulous color descriptions have played an important role in setting the records right. The expertly hand-colored copper plate illustrations are extraordinarily beautiful and of value to science to the present day.

These volumes formed part of Robert L. Stuart's bequest to the American Museum of Natural History. The Stuart Library, comprising more than 10,000 volumes, was the largest private collection of books in America by the late nineteenth century and included books "unsurpassed in the brilliancy or coloration, drawings, and impressions" (*New York Times*, 1885).

2. *Panulirus homarus* (Linnaeus, 1758) (*Cancer* [*Astacus*] *homarus*, Herbst). The scalloped spiny lobster, a nocturnal, social, reef-dwelling species, is widely distributed in the Indo West Pacific Ocean.

3. *Portunus* (*Portunus*) *pelagicus* (Linnaeus, 1758) (*Cancer cedonulli*, Herbst, 1794). Recorded throughout East Asia, this species is found in shallow sandy and muddy lagoons and estuaries.

4. Left: *Charybdis Charybdis feriata* (Linnaeus, 1758) (*Cancer cruciatus*, Herbst, 1794). Herbst's name *cruciata* refers to the image of the cross on its carapace. Middle: *Scylla olivacea* (Herbst, 1794) (*Cancer olivaceus*, Herbst, 1794). The orange mud crab is associated with mangrove ecosystems throughout the Indo West Pacific region.

5. *Zosimus aeneus* (Linnaeus, 1758) (*Cancer amphitrite*, Herbst, 1801). Widely distributed throughout the Indo Pacific and common on reef flats, both its shell and meat contain neurotoxins and its poison can be fatal.

Bella Galil *is a research associate in the Division of Invertebrate Zoology at the American Museum of Natural History and a senior scientist at the National Institute of Oceanography in Haifa, Israel.*

1. Lai, "A Revision of the *Portunus pelagicus* (Linnaeus, 1758) species complex (Crustacea: Brachyura: Portunidae), with the recognition of four species. Raffles Bulletin of Zoology," 199–237.

3.

4.

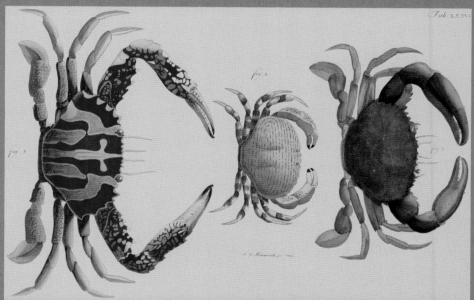

5.

Tab. XL.

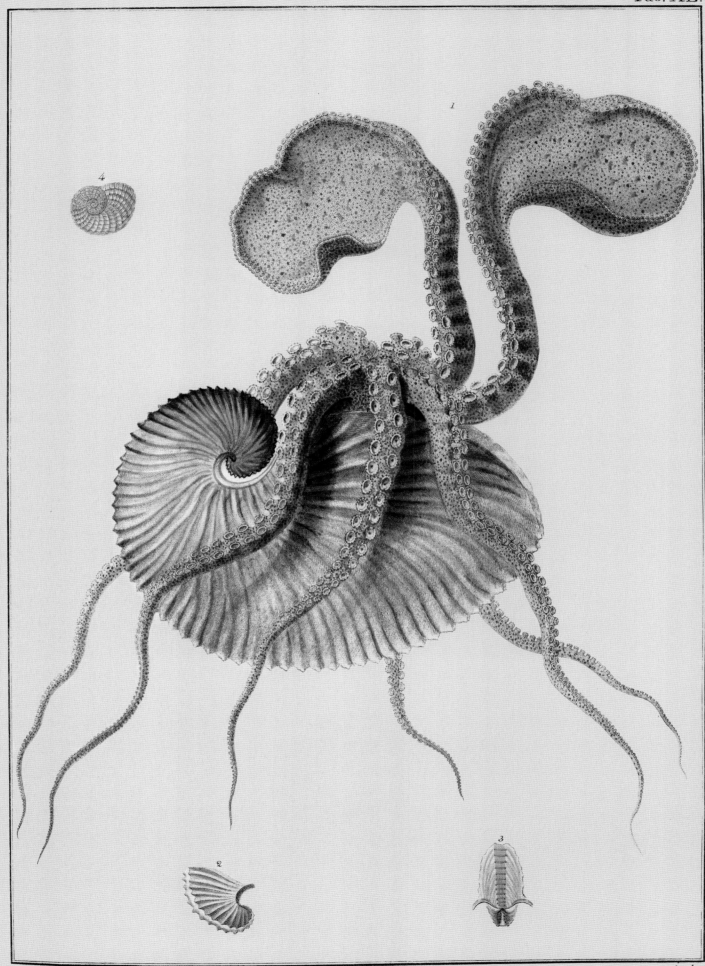

Morelli, et Siesto del.

Cataneo, et Toro Sculp

At the Dawn of Malacology: The Salient and Silent Oeuvre of Giuseppe Saverio Poli

ILYA TËMKIN

Author

Giuseppe Saverio Poli
(1746–1825)

Title

*Testacea utriusque Siciliae
eorumque historia et anatome*

*(Shelled animals of the Two
Sicilies with their description
and anatomy)*

Imprint

Parma: [Giambatista Bodoni],
1791–1827

Testacea utriusque Siciliae eorumque historia et anatome (*Shelled animals of the Two Sicilies with their description and anatomy*) is one of the most exquisitely illustrated and lavishly published treatises on mollusks. This work stands out not only as a monument of typographic art, but also as being far ahead of its time scientifically. Its significant insights were largely unknown to contemporary science. Such a fate for the book—destined to become a sought-after bibliographical rarity—was due to the author's remarkable power of observation and to the turbulent period of European history at the brink of the nineteenth century.

Giuseppe Saverio Poli was born in 1746, and studied classics, theology, and natural sciences at the University of Padua. After appointment to a post at the Royal Military Academy in 1774, he traveled to London to study military institutions and to acquire scientific instruments for the academy. There he met Captain James Cook and naturalist Sir Joseph Banks, from whom he acquired fossils and other specimens from the Pacific Islands. Poli also befriended William Hunter, a famous English physician and collector, who suggested Poli study the mollusks of the Mediterranean Sea. During his travels, Poli made acquaintance with other renowned European naturalists and collected natural objects and cultural artifacts for his private collection. During the 1806 conquest of Naples by the French, the collection was plundered of rare specimens. (Remaining specimens are now at the Museo di Storia Naturale in Naples. A collection of Poli's wax models of molluscan anatomy is presently housed at the Muséum National d'Histoire Naturelle in Paris, and some of the models match specimens figured in plates in *Testacea utriusque Siciliae*.) Despite his multiple academic and administrative positions and tutoring service for the crown prince of Naples, Poli pursued diverse scientific interests until his death in 1825.

Poli's reputation in natural history rests upon the *Testacea utriusque Siciliae*, an outstanding work on comparative anatomy and classification of mollusks of Naples and Sicily. The first two volumes were published under Poli's supervision in 1791 and 1795. The third volume was nearly completed when civil war erupted in 1799. It was published posthumously in two parts. The first part indicated Poli as author but included annotations by Stefano Delle Chiaje. The second part, written by Delle Chiaje, presented an account of the species illustrated but not described by Poli. All volumes were published in folio format in Parma by Giambatista Bodoni, one of the most important Italian printers of the day. The engraved colored plates had matching line-drawing versions with labels.

Testacea utriusque Siciliae was a groundbreaking work in the study of mollusks. First, it established molluscan comparative anatomy as a distinct discipline. Until Poli's oeuvre, the study of mollusks was based largely on shells. Poli recognized

1. External morphology of a female paper nautilus, *Argonauta argo*, with the egg case.

2.

that soft tissues provide a wealth of information for classification, and documented various aspects of morphology with exceptional accuracy. Many of the characters discovered by Poli were new to science. For example, Poli was the first author who recognized structures on mantle edge of some bivalve mollusks as eyes.

Second, *Testacea utriusque Siciliae* was the first treatise on molluscan biochemistry and physiology. Poli invented an apparatus to measure the contractile force of adductor muscles, injected mercury into the vessels to trace blood flow, and set up breeding chambers to study molluscan reproduction and development. He investigated the composition of blood, described the crystalline structure and chemical composition of the shell, and identified the crystalline style as a structure related to digestion.

Third, *Testacea utriusque Siciliae* offered a novel system for classifying mollusks. Poli was the first author to propose a classification based entirely on soft anatomical characteristics. Because such classification was at odds with the prevailing shell-based system, Poli developed two independent systems of nomenclature, one for the names of the shells and the other for the names of the soft body. Both systems followed the Linnaean binomial principle. In this classification, genus names were based on anatomical characteristics, but corresponding shells were referred to by names composed by compounding the word *derma* ("skin" in Greek) to the genus name. For example, an animal of the genus *Cerastes* "inhabits" the *Cerastoderma* shell. While Poli's classification was never applied, a number of his scientific names remain valid to this day.

Despite the fact that *Testacea utriusque Siciliae* established Poli's reputation as the father of malacology (the study of mollusks), it did not enjoy the wide recognition it deserved. This was partly due to politics, as the ties between Italy and France (the centers of natural sciences at the time) were severed in the aftermath of the Napoleonic wars. It was also due to limited circulation because of high publication costs. Despite these factors, the wealth of anatomical data from *Testacea utriusque Siciliae* fueled works of future generations of malacologists.

2. Hand-colored portrait of G. S. Poli from *Testacea utriusque Siciliae.*

3. Scientific instruments used by G. S. Poli, including dissecting tools, microscopes, and an apparatus to measure the contractile force of adductor muscles of clams.

4. Overview of the external morphology (with shell removed) and detailed dissections of soft parts of a Mediterranean pen shell, *Pinna nobilis.*

5. Shell morphology and aspects of external and internal anatomy of a Mediterranean scallop, *Pecten jacobaeus.*

6. The corresponding line drawing provides labels for morphological characters discussed in detail in the legend and corresponding chapter of the book.

Ilya Tёmkin is a research associate in the Division of Paleontology at the American Museum of Natural History and an assistant professor in the Biology Department at Northern Virginia Community College in Annandale, Virginia.

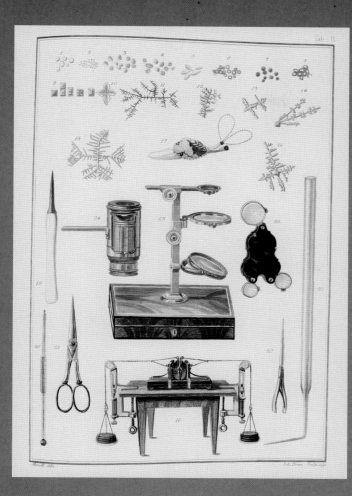

Tab. II.

3.

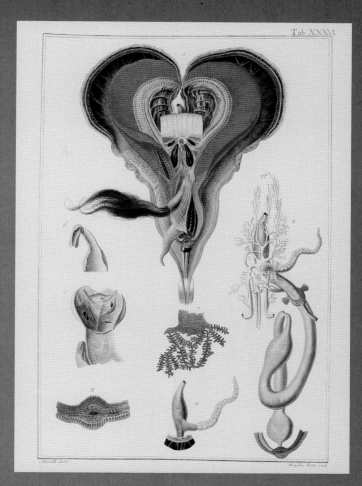

Tab. XXXVI.

4.

Tab. XXVII.

5.

Tab. XXVII.

6.

Pith Paper Butterfly Souvenirs

DIANA SHIH

Author
Anonymous

Title
Chinese plates of butterflies

Imprint
China: ca. 1830–1871

1. This album features over a hundred minutely hand-painted butterflies. Unlike most of the works in this book, whose purpose it is to represent and describe the natural world as accurately as possible, this volume was created solely as a fanciful representation of already colorful creatures.

This little gem was donated to the American Museum of Natural History in 1920 by Mrs. Catharine A. Malcomson, who had received it as a gift from the well-known East India merchant Fletcher Westray half a century earlier. It is a beautiful example of what is known as Chinese trade art. Chinese export watercolors were painted in the port cities of Hong Kong, Macao, and Canton and sold to Western customers in the mid-nineteenth century. Many, like this one, were painted on a type of paper unique to this genre, called pith paper.

Pith paper is not traditional paper—which is made of matted layers of macerated fibers—but is made, instead, from the soft, fibrous material found on the inside branches of the small tree *Tetrapanax papyriferus*, commonly known as rice paper plant. Rice paper plant is a misnomer, as rice paper is *not* pith paper (rice paper, however, is made from the rice plant). The fibrous plant material is collected by pushing a circular dowel through harvested plant branches that have soaked in water for several days. The resulting extracted material is then dried and cut into thin slices using a very sharp knife. Cutting requires great skill, and the constraints of the process mean that the finished sheets used for painting seldom, if ever, measure more than 12 by 8 inches. The finished product is a soft, almost translucent piece of paper that is perfect for the production of miniature paintings using watercolors and gouache—mediums that when applied to pith paper appear to float on the paper's surface while also allowing its unique texture to shine through.

One of the remarkable properties of pith paper is its ability to retain color vividly—and for a long time, as seen here. The paper also attests to the skills of the painters, because once color is applied to pith paper it cannot be erased, nor can the finished painting be altered with over-painting. The colors used were those common in Chinese painting, but there was also a tendency for primary colors to predominate. The watercolors were painted in workshops using mass-production techniques, so authorship cannot be ascertained. However, this album may be attributed to an artist named Youqua, who flourished in Canton between 1840 and 1870.

These works are interesting not only because of the materials used to create them, but also because they are specific to a significant period in Chinese history. These "souvenirs" were the direct results of the aftermath of the Opium War, which China lost in 1842, and which resulted in the English setting up several trading posts in China. The China trade flourished until the beginning of the twentieth century.

Pith paper presumably came into use for painting to satisfy the increasing demand for small, inexpensive, and easily transported souvenirs. Paintings in oils, on board and canvas, were highly prized but were costly and difficult to carry home. Albums of pith paintings, on the other hand, were inexpensive, light, easy to pack,

2.

and gave the pictures some protection on the long voyage home. Because the paintings were sold bound into albums—and therefore protected from the light—they retain their bright colors to this day. Illustrations of everyday Chinese life, courtiers, and landscapes were very popular, but other topics included birds, fishes, and butterflies rendered in various degrees of fancifulness.

The illustrations are not scientifically accurate, but were meant to amuse the viewer with images of the exotic East. Developed to appeal to Westerners unfamiliar with Chinese culture, paintings on pith were produced by artisans rather than by the intellectual elite, and were therefore not accepted by the Chinese as "high" Chinese art. As a result, such paintings are rarely preserved in fine-art museums in the West, making this treasure from our collection all the more prized and cherished.

2., 3., 4. & 5. Four plates of more colorful butterflies.

Diana Shih is the Assistant Director for Bibliographic Records Management in the Research Library at the American Museum of Natural History.

3.

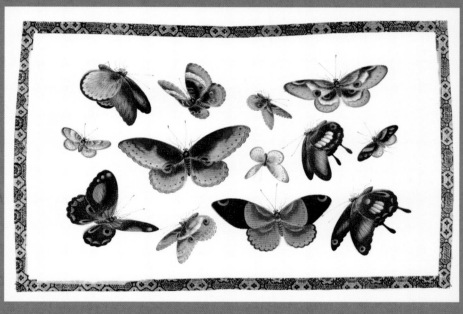

4.

5.

Alexander Wilson and the Birth of American Ornithology

MAI QARAMAN REITMEYER

Author

Alexander Wilson
(1766–1813)

Title

*American ornithology, or
the natural history of the birds
of the United States*

Imprint

Philadelphia: Bradford and
Inskeep, 1808–1824

Alexander Wilson, often called the father of American ornithology, created the first scientific treatise of American birds, representing 264 of the 363 species found in North America. Of these, thirty-nine were new to science, and twenty-three others were sufficiently described to differentiate them from the European species with which they had been previously confused.

Alexander Wilson was born July 6, 1766, in Paisley, Scotland. He attended grammar school until his mother died in 1779, after which he was apprenticed to William Duncan, a weaver. While at the loom, he began writing poems and stories. During the seven years that he worked for Duncan, Wilson became very critical of the labor conditions and, after leaving the loom, published a piece of satire that was judged as libel by local manufacturers. He had become increasingly dissatisfied with Scotland, and after a short imprisonment for the libel suit, he decided to leave for America. Wilson arrived after fifty-three days aboard a ship from Belfast to New Castle. From Delaware, Wilson continued on foot to Philadelphia and was captivated by the strange birds and new trees and flowers he saw along the way.

Upon arrival in Philadelphia, Wilson worked many jobs, but it was his eventual employment as a schoolmaster at Gray's Ferry, outside of Philadelphia, that would set the stage for him to become a well-known figure in the world of American ornithology. While at Gray's Ferry, he befriended his neighbor, the famous naturalist William Bartram. Wilson spent much time in Bartram's library studying works of Mark Catesby, George Edwards, and other famous European ornithologists. Wilson had traveled through northeastern America on foot in the years since he had arrived and felt that he had learned American birds well enough to detect errors in these authors' works. It was then that he decided that he would publish his own book on American birds, and illustrate it with his own drawings. Alexander Lawson, a fellow Scotsman and well-known engraver, tutored him in drawing. When he wasn't working, Wilson spent all available daylight hours in the field collecting specimens, and nights drawing and painting by candlelight. Wilson shared his findings and submitted his drawings to Bartram for advice and criticism.

In 1804, Wilson set out on a two-month journey to Niagara Falls in search of more birds to describe and paint. He sent several of his drawings to Thomas Jefferson, who offered Wilson thanks. Wilson wrote to Jefferson again to make a case for himself as a collector on Jefferson's Zebulon Pike Expedition to the Mississippi in 1806. Unfortunately, this letter was never received, and Wilson was not appointed to the expedition.

However, his luck was about to change. A few months later, Wilson found employment with the publisher Samuel Bradford, as assistant editor for Rees's New

1. "Kingfisher." Typical of
works produced in the early
nineteenth century, Wilson's
paintings usually illustrated
birds in profile, with little or
no background.

77

2.

3.

2. "Owl Copper." The engraver Alexander Lawson transferred Wilson's drawings to copper plates, which were then printed and hand colored by artists.

3. "Owl." Due to his small budget, Wilson had to include as many specimens as possible on each plate. These economical arrangements give his plates a signature look.

4. "Carolina Parakeet." Wilson described the now-extinct Carolina parakeet in 1832. Once common in the southeastern United States, it became increasingly scarce as deforestation reduced its habitat.

5. Wilson's description of the breeding grounds of the Great Heron vividly described the tall, dense Atlantic white cedar swamps of southern New Jersey. Less than a century later, these swamps had disappeared due to clear-cutting Atlantic white cedar.

6. "Passenger Pigeon." Wilson also described enormous colonies of the extinct passenger pigeon. It is thought that their large numbers allowed them to overwhelm their predators. Overhunting reduced their colonies to the point that they were no longer able to nest in these vast colonies, which in turn led to their demise.

Cyclopedia, "a universal dictionary of the arts and sciences." Wilson shared his plans for *American ornithology* with Bradford, who enthusiastically agreed to publish the volumes as long as Wilson financed the project with a subscription service. Such a publishing structure was typical for many works and especially so for illustrated natural history volumes of this time. The author or publisher would essentially identify a number of paying customers prior to the printing of a set number of copies, thus ensuring a solvent enterprise.

Lawson was hired as the principal engraver of Wilson's works, and in September 1808, Volume 1 of *American ornithology* was complete. Lawson combined etching with line engraving in his copper plates, and each print was hand colored with watercolors. In the subsequent few years, Wilson devoted all his free time to working on *American ornithology* and traveled throughout the country to gather both specimens and subscribers for his publication.

Wilson intended *American ornithology* to be a ten-volume work, six with land birds and four with water birds. Unfortunately, Wilson had only nearly completed the eighth volume when he faced his untimely death due to dysentery at age forty-seven. George Ord, Wilson's friend and executor, took it upon himself to finish the series. Later editions and reprints appeared throughout the nineteenth century, but while Wilson had published his birds in the order that he collected them, later editions were arranged by taxonomic group. Additionally, Charles Lucien Bonaparte, Napoleon's nephew and an ornithologist, published a four-volume continuation of Wilson's work describing birds "not given by Wilson." These volumes were also engraved by Lawson and based on illustrations by Titian Ramsey Peale.

Few errors have been found in Wilson's *American ornithology* since it was originally published. In addition to being aesthetically pleasing, his *American ornithology* contains reliable accounts of migration patterns and bird behavior, and documents four species that are now extinct, making it an invaluable scientific work still, even two centuries after its publication.

Mai Qaraman Reitmeyer *is the Research Services Librarian in the Research Library at the American Museum of Natural History.*

4.

1. Carolina Parrot. 2. Canada Flycatcher. 3. Hooded F. 4. Green black capt F.
26

5.

1. Yellow crowned Heron. 2. Great Heron. 3. American Bittern. 4. Least H.

6.

DÉTAILS D'ARCHITECTURE DU GRAND TEMPLE.

Egypt Revealed

NINA J. ROOT

Title
Description de l'Egypte, ou recueil des observations et des recherches qui ont été faites en Egypte pendant l'expédition de l'armée francaise

(Description of Egypt, or a compilation of observations and research made in Egypt during the expedition of the French army)

Imprint
Paris: Imprimerie de C. L. F. Panckoucke, 1820–1830

1. These are the capitals of the columns in the colonnade of the Grand Temple of Horus at Apollinopolis (now Edfou). The temple is dedicated to the falcon-headed god, Horus, and was built by Ptolomey.

The publication of the landmark, outsized *Description de l'Egypte* (*Description of Egypt*) was decreed by Napoleon Bonaparte in 1802. This seminal publication on Egyptology was a collaborative effort of some 150 prominent French scientists and scholars and 2,000 technicians and artists. It is the record of Napoleon Bonaparte's Scientific and Artistic Commission that accompanied the ill-fated French expedition to Egypt (1798–1801).

On the morning of May 19, 1798, Napoleon Bonaparte, aboard the French flagship *L'Orient,* signaled his armada in Toulon Harbor to set sail. For eight hours, 180 vessels with 17,000 troops, 15,000 sailors, and a scientific and artistic commission of 167 civilians sailed past Bonaparte's flagship to a secret destination. Napoleon, supreme commander of the French army and navy, was just twenty-nine as he watched his armada sail for Egypt. The commission of 167 civilians—whose mean age was twenty-five—included engineers, musicians, artists, scientists, interpreters, printers, literary figures, architects, physicists, naturalists, chemists, philosophers, cartographers, and physicians. Their mission was to learn all they possibly could about Egypt, Syria, Turkey, and Islam. Baron Dominique Vivant Denon, an artist and eventual director of the Louvre Museum, was the leader of the commission and was the oldest member, at fifty-one.

Although illness, battles, heat, hunger, privation, and death plagued the soldiers and civilians in Cairo, the commissioners were able to explore and sketch the ancient Pharaonic ruins, collect local fauna and flora, study Egypt's laws and customs, and map Egypt and its adjacent countries. More important, they established the Institute of Egypt for the progress and propagation of the sciences, and to research, study, and publish natural, industrial, and historical data on Egypt. Napoleon named himself vice president, and the members established presses and published a scientific periodical, *La Decade Egyptienne,* and a newspaper, *Courrier de l'Egypte.*

The headquarters of the Institute of Egypt was in a Cairo suburb, in the Palace of Quassim Bey. The institute included beautiful gardens in which to study botany; an aviary and a zoo; a chemical laboratory; and a library and museum of natural history, archaeology, and minerals. It was the precursor of the present-day, extraordinary Cairo Museum. Informal gatherings of between forty and fifty people took place every evening in the garden to discuss travel plans, discoveries, ancient Egypt, and the mores of the Egyptians. Generals, Napoleon, high Egyptian officials, and sheiks often joined the nightly discussions. One evening, after a presentation on the fish of the Nile by the naturalist Goeffroy St. Hilaire (the eventual director of the Muséum National d'Histoire Naturelle in Paris), a sheik pointed out the vanity of

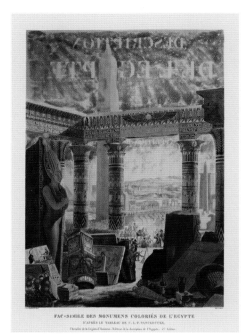

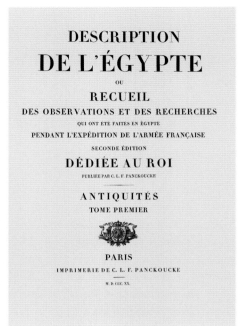

DESCRIPTION
DE L'ÉGYPTE
OU
RECUEIL
DES OBSERVATIONS ET DES RECHERCHES
QUI ONT ÉTÉ FAITES EN ÉGYPTE
PENDANT L'EXPÉDITION DE L'ARMÉE FRANÇAISE
SECONDE ÉDITION
DÉDIÉE AU ROI
PUBLIÉE PAR C. L. F. PANCKOUCKE

ANTIQUITÉS
TOME PREMIER

PARIS
IMPRIMERIE DE C. L. F. PANCKOUCKE

M. D. CCC. XX.

2.

FAC-SIMILE DES MONUMENS COLORIÉS DE L'ÉGYPTE
D'APRÈS LE TABLEAU DE C. L. F. PANCKOUCKE
Chevalier de la Légion d'honneur . Éditeur de la Description de l'Égypte . 27. Kolom .

2. The paint used in the frontispiece's blue sky contained white lead watercolor, which has become discolored by a chemical reaction with the atmosphere. The large printed letters of the title on the facing page have inhibited this reaction, leaving the colors untouched and the letters' images in reverse.

3. The felucca has been the mode of transportation on the Nile for millennia. It is characterized by the lateen (triangular) sail, and can still be seen on the Nile and throughout the Middle East. The scene on the bank shows the irrigation system that helped grow the food that fed Egypt. A similar system can still be seen as one travels along the modern-day Nile.

4. The bird mummies in this plate were found in Thebes and include the African sacred ibis (*Threskiornis aethiopicus*) at top; the merlin (*Falco columbarius*) at right; and the Northern goshawk (*Accipiter gentilis*) at left. The cat skeleton, at the bottom, came from a mummy found in Saqqara, where cat mummies were prepared as carefully as human mummies.

5. The Colossi of Memnon (Thebes) are 60-foot-high stone statues of Amenhotep III that have stood across the Nile from Luxor since 1350 B.C. Two smaller figures beside the legs are of his wife Tiy and mother Mutenwiya. Side panels show relief images of the Nile god Hapy. They guarded the entrance to Amenhotep's mortuary temple.

such research, since the Prophet had declared that God had created 30,000 species: 10,000 inhabited land and air, and 20,000 in water.

Napoleon abandoned the expedition and for political reasons returned to France, leaving the scholars and the army to follow. When the scholars asked to return to France with their collections along with the departing officers and navy, France was already at war with Great Britain, and a British naval blockade thwarted their departure. Eventually, a treaty of capitulation was signed in which the British demanded that all the collections be turned over as the spoils of war, including the Rosetta stone, which had been discovered in 1799. Geoffroy St. Hilaire declared that the scholars would rather follow their collections to England than give them up. The British finally allowed the commissioners to keep their intellectual property (drawings, notes, and collections). The Rosetta stone and other antiquities were turned over to the British Museum.

The scholars finally were repatriated in 1801, and set out to publish *Description de l'Egypte.* An enormous body of material, reports, notes, illustrations, plans, and maps had to be organized, text written and edited, type set, 837 illustrations engraved, and the volumes designed, printed, and bound. Three thousand reams of Grand Jesus sheets (large folio single sheets) were used. To print the extraordinary outsized plates, Nicholas Jacques Conte, inventor of the graphite pencil and member of the commission, invented a printing machine that revolutionized the engraving trade. The copper plates are preserved in the Louvre. Edme François Jomard, cartographer and archaeologist, served as general editor. All the plates in the rare first edition are colored except the frontispiece, while the plates in the second edition are uncolored except for the frontispiece. The scholars' most important contributions were their findings related to the region's geography, the establishment of modern Egyptology, the founding of what is now the Cairo Museum, and the publication of the *Description de l'Egypte.*

Nina J. Root *is the Director Emerita of the Research Library at the American Museum of Natural History.*

VUES ET DÉTAILS DE DEUX MACHINES À ARROSER, APPELÉES CHÂDOUF ET MENTÂL.

3.

MOMIES D'OISEAUX ET SQUELETTES DE MOMIES.

4.

VUE DES DEUX COLOSSES.

5.

Lachesis rhombeata.

Prince Maximilian zu Wied: A Military Man Turned Naturalist

CHARLES W. MYERS

Author
Prince Maximilian zu Wied
(1782–1867)

Title
*Abbildungen zur
Naturgeschichte Brasiliens*

*(Illustrations to the natural
history of Brazil)*

Imprint
Weimar: im Verlage des
Grossherzogl. Sächs. priv.
Landes-Industrie-Comptoirs,
1822–1831

Prince Maximilian zu Wied was a military leader during the Napoleonic era, serving with distinction as a major in the Prussian cavalry. Wied's passion since youth, however, was natural history, and he eventually met and came under the influence of Alexander von Humboldt, renowned naturalist and South American explorer. Wied wanted to make an expedition to Brazil, a country that had been politically off limits to his mentor Humboldt. Wied's chance for travel came after Napoleon's defeat in 1814, and he quickly made ready for his South American adventure. Although Napoleon returned to the battlefield in 1815, the prince was by then in Brazil, where he much later learned of Napoleon's final defeat at Waterloo.

Wied traveled extensively through wilderness along the Atlantic coast of Brazil, observing native peoples and making important collections of reptiles, amphibians, birds, and mammals. He presented the scientific results principally in three classic works: The first two-volume *Reise nach Brasilien in den Jahren 1815 bis 1817 (Travel in Brazil in the years 1815 to 1817)*, published between 1820 and 1821, is a diary of the expedition and includes descriptions of some new species in footnotes. Early English translations of this work were printed in London, and found an audience eager to read about the wonders of the New World. The second four-volume *Beiträge zur Naturgeschichte von Brasilien (Contributions to the natural history of Brazil)*, published between 1825 and 1833, is a meticulous taxonomic review of all the species collected by Wied; the first volume of the *Beiträge* is devoted to reptiles and amphibians.

Wied's third major contribution from his Brazilian expedition is the *Abbildungen zur Naturgeschichte Brasiliens (Illustrations to the natural history of Brazil)*, a collection of ninety hand-painted copper plates usually found bound in a single volume. This rare work was irregularly published over the period of years from 1822 to 1831 in a series of fifteen issues, each in a printed cover with six folio plates of Brazilian animals accompanied by short texts in German and French. Although the individual plates were not numbered, some libraries assigned penciled numbers to the plates in the order of binding, which varies among institutions—these fictitious numbers sometimes are cited as original data in bibliographic references to individual plates. The original printed covers and a few plates often are lacking in the bound volumes. (The American Museum of Natural History's copy lacks two herpetological plates and all but one cover.)

Wied oversaw preparation of the *Abbildungen* plates in Germany. He had been well aware that bright colorations of many amphibians and reptiles fade quickly in preservative, so he capably illustrated many animals in the field with pen-and-watercolor sketches. Artists later worked from the preserved animals as posed in the

1. The *Lachesis muta rhombeata* (Wied) is a dangerous bushmaster from the Atlantic Forest of Brazil.

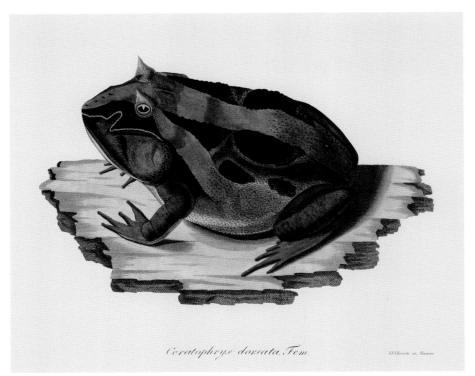

2.

Ceratophrys dorsata. Fem.

2. Pictured is the horned frog *Ceratophrys aurita* (Raddi, 1823). Wied named the genus *Ceratophrys* in 1824, but placement of Raddi's earlier name *Bufo auritus* in that genus replaced Wied's synonymous species names *dorsata* and *varius*.

3. A false coral snake named *Oxyrhopus formosus* (Wied).

4. A large, semiarboreal, bird-eating snake currently known as *Pseustes sulphureus poecilostoma* (Wied).

5. In this composite plate, Wied was understandably misled into thinking that he had two new lizards, which he named *Anolis gracilis* and *Anolis viridis*. The upper figure shows a male displaying with extended dewlap. The lower figure is a female; the sexual dimorphism is extraordinary. Both species names were coined by Wied in 1821, but are now recognized as synonyms of the earlier-named *Anolis punctatus* (Daudin, 1802).

prince's drawings to prepare new paintings for transfer to copper plate. Taxonomic details, including scalation, came from the specimens as well as color from Wied's watercolors and notes. Color was recopied by hand from the artists' paintings onto each printed plate. These illustrations accurately show details of scale and color-pattern variations and often allow an investigator to determine which of a series of specimens was figured. In a few cases showing bilateral asymmetry in scales or pattern, one can see that the painting was transferred to copper plate in mirror image, which was commonplace for early engravings. In at least one case, however, an extra step was taken to retain the original orientation of a lizard.

After finishing his studies of the Brazilian material, Prince Maximilian undertook his more famous North American expedition, sailing to Boston in 1832 and exploring along the Missouri River between 1833 and 1834. He hired Karl (Charles) Bodmer, a skilled watercolorist, to travel along and paint Native Americans. Wied's engaging account of the expedition and Bodmer's breathtaking watercolors preserved knowledge of a people soon to be extirpated by introduced disease. After his death, the bulk of Wied's zoological collection was purchased for the American Museum of Natural History.

There is lingering confusion as to how Prince Maximilian's name should be cited. He used the compound name "Wied-Neuwied" for all works published before 1825. The family Wied-Neuwied inherited the estate of Wied-Runkel in 1824, and geographic modifiers of the Wied name were officially dropped. The prince did not use "Wied-Neuwied" after 1824, except (for editorial continuity) in the *Abbildungen*. The latest form of his name—*Wied, Maximilian, Prinz zu*—is correct usage following modern cataloging rules, and the prince's own preference. The noble preposition *von* sometimes is used in Wied's name, but *zu* was the family's predicate of choice for centuries.

Charles W. Myers *is a curator emeritus in the Herpetology Department in the Division of Vertebrate Zoology at the American Museum of Natural History.*

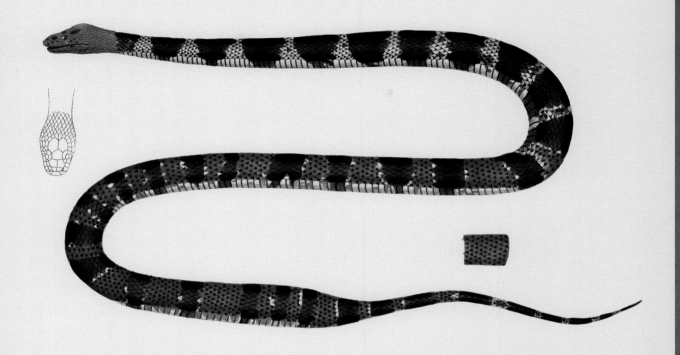

Coluber formosus.

3.

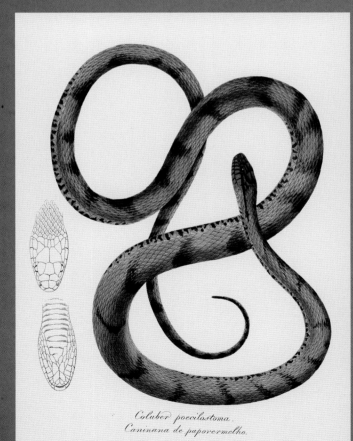

Coluber poecilostoma.
Caninana de papovermelho.

4.

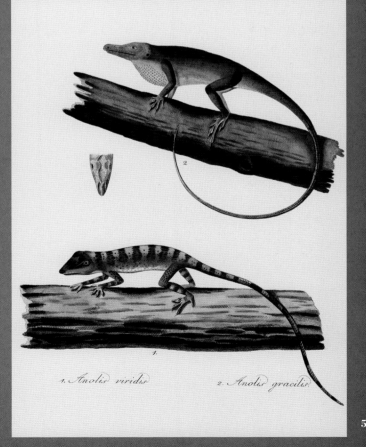

1. *Anolis viridis*   2. *Anolis gracilis.*

5.

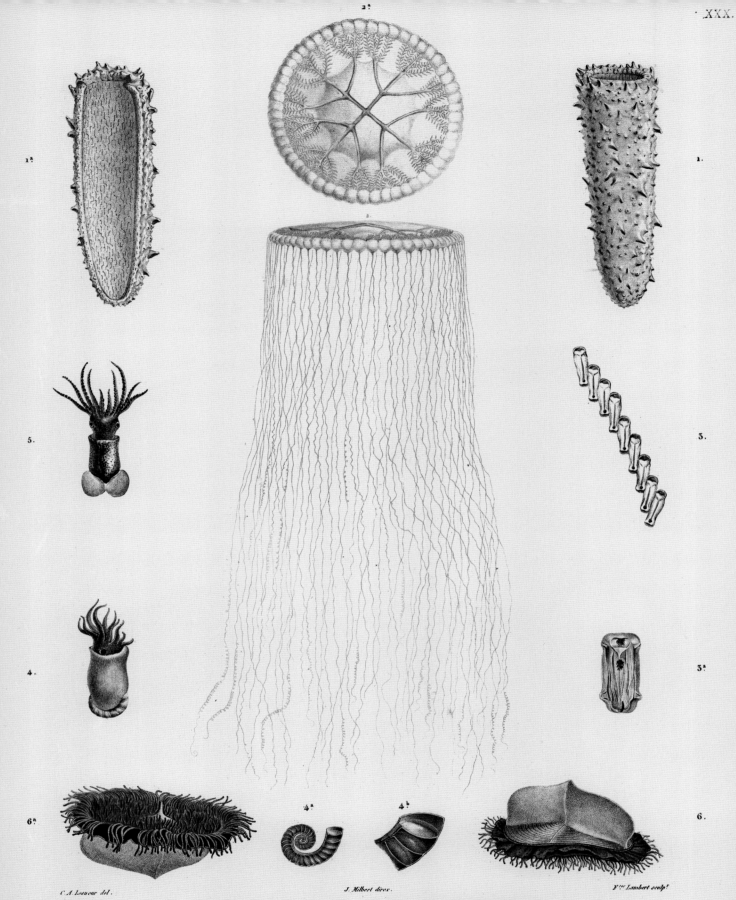

C.A.Lesueur del.   J. Milbert direx.   F.ço. Lambert sculp.t

MOLLUSQUES ET ZOOPHYTES.

1. PYROSOMA *Atlanticum*. N.   1.ᵃ *Coupe longitudinale du* PYROSOMA.   4. SPIRULEA *Prototypos*. N.   4.ᵃ *Coupe du test*. 4.ᵇ *Portion grossie*.

2. CUVIERIA *Carisochroma*. N.   2.ᵃ CUVIERIA *Vue en dessus*.   5. LOLIGO *Cardioptera*. N.   5. CALMAR *Cardioptère*. N.

3. SALPA *Cyanogaster*. N.   3.ᵃ SALPA *Antheliophora*. N.   6. VELELLA *Scaphidia*. N. (*dessus*)   6.ᵃ VELELLA *Scaphidia*. N. (*dessous*)

De l'Imprimerie de Langlois.

Discovering a New World:
François Péron's Voyage to Australia

RICHARD PEARSON

Author

François Péron (1775–1810)

Title

*Voyage de découvertes aux
terres australes: fait par ordre
du gouvernement, sur les
corvettes le Géographe,
le Naturaliste, et la goëlette
le Casuarina, pendant les
années 1800, 1801, 1802,
1803, et 1804*

*(Voyage of discovery to the
southern lands: made by
government order, on the
corvettes Le Géographe, Le
Naturaliste, and the schooner
Le Casuarina, during the years
1800, 1801, 1802, 1803,
and 1804)*

Imprint

Paris: Imprimerie Impériale,
1807–1816

1. A selection of mollusks
and "zoophytes." Péron was
fascinated and confused by
these animals, questioning what
he should make of the species
shown here, "which exhibit no
apparent means of movement,
digestions, respiration, or even
reproduction and yet cover the
sea in countless swarms."

After completing school in 1790 at age fifteen, fighting in the French Revolution, and then studying medicine and zoology in Paris, François Péron seemed destined for a successful career in the French capital. Yet a seemingly impulsive move—most likely driven by turmoil over rejection of a proposal of marriage—saw Péron enlist as part of the scientific team that was to join a lengthy voyage of discovery to the southern lands. Commissioned by Napoleon Bonaparte, and under the captaincy of Nicolas Baudin, the expedition set sail from Le Havre, France, on October 19, 1800, with two vessels: *Le Géographe* and *Le Naturaliste*.

The primary mission for Baudin's expedition was to chart the Australian coastline, significant chunks of which remained unmapped three decades after Captain James Cook led the first European voyage to locate the continent's eastern coastline. In particular, the south coast remained unknown, yet Baudin would be beaten to much of the discovery by the young English captain Matthew Flinders. France and England were at war at the time, and on receiving word of the French voyage, the English had hastily launched Flinders's competing effort out of fear that the French might be secretly planning an Australian colony. Nonetheless, in the early months of 1802, Baudin was first to explore the two hundred miles of coast between Encounter Bay in the west and Cape Banks in the east. A year later, Baudin's expedition was first to chart the south coast of Kangaroo Island. Many of the expedition's names for landmarks still remain to this day, including Cape Reaumur, Cape Duquesne, and Descartes Bay.

For François Péron, the voyage was much more about discovering and naming species than it was about naming landmarks. The Australian flora and fauna remained largely mysterious—they were the naturalist's equivalent of uncharted waters. Péron and his colleagues vociferously set about collecting and studying the plants and animals of the places they visited, as well as observing native peoples whenever possible. On Kangaroo Island, for instance, Péron collected 336 species of a wide variety of creatures, including spiders, insects, worms, lizards, and starfish. Many of his collections were of previously unknown species. During just two weeks on King Island, Péron and artist Charles-Alexandre Lesueur collected at least fifteen new species, including sponges, tube worms, mollusks, and an acorn barnacle. Here, Péron also collected the type specimen of a clawless lobster, which was later named *Ibacus péronii* in his honor by an English zoologist. By the time the voyage returned to France, the scientists had collected so many cases of specimens—including preserved reptiles, shells, dried plants, six hundred types of seeds, seventy large boxes of living plants, and roughly one hundred live animals—that unloading the ship took two weeks.

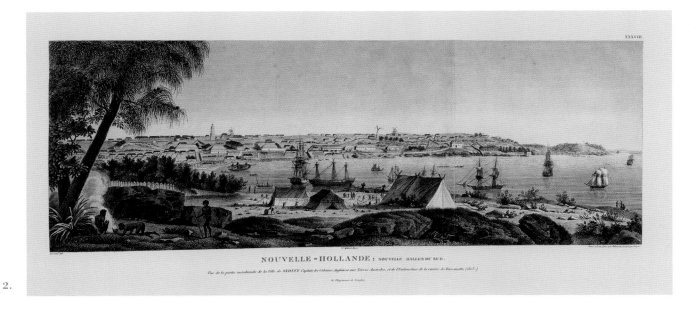

NOUVELLE - HOLLANDE : NOUVELLE GALLES DU SUD.

Vue de la partie méridionale de la Ville de SYDNEY Capitale des Colonies Anglaises aux Terres Australes, et de l'embouchure de la rivière de Parramatta (1803.)

2.

Péron's writings reveal a sharp, scientific mind. He recognized a basic tenet of biogeography, that species "are established in certain regions, and it is there that they are most numerous," and he made reference to differentiation within species, which is central to the process of natural selection: "I have found important differences between the least dissimilar of those creatures that are supposed to be of identical species." Péron's thinking was no doubt influenced by the early evolutionary theories of Jean-Baptiste Lamarck, whose lectures he had attended while in Paris, yet it would be another half century before Charles Darwin and Alfred Russell Wallace finally solved the great puzzle that helped make sense of Péron's observations.

At a time when society was only beginning to come to grips with the concept that species in God's creation could go extinct, Péron was especially insightful in his concern over the human impact on nature. Writing about King Island, Péron noted that animals had "no notion of flight or self-defense" such that hunting on the island "would have been sufficient to destroy the whole stock of these innocent animals." As the Australian historian Edward Duyker has noted, a distinctive subspecies of emu that was once endemic to the island is now extinct.

The Baudin expedition returned to France on March 25, 1804, without its captain, who died of tuberculosis during the trip home. Baudin's death left Péron to write the official account of the voyage, which reveals a significant amount of animosity between the captain and the naturalist. Péron's version of events was published between 1807 and 1816 in two volumes of text and an atlas in two parts, though Péron died in 1810, at age thirty-five, leaving a fellow survivor of the voyage, Louis de Freycinet, to complete the second volume. The atlas includes many stunning plates, including charts and color drawings of landscapes, native peoples, and, of course, a great variety of species. Perhaps of most historical significance, because Flinders's return to England was delayed until 1810, due to his imprisonment in Mauritius, the first complete, detailed chart of the entire Australian continent, including the recently explored southern coast, was published in Péron's volume.

2. The harbor town that would become Sydney, as it was during Péron's visit in 1803.

3. Adult male (left), adult female (center), and young cassowary from Kangaroo Island, named "Ile Decrès" by Péron.

4. The first published, complete, detailed chart of the full Australian continent, including the southern coastline that was explored by the Baudin/Péron voyage.

Richard Pearson is the Director of Biodiversity Informatics Research in the Center for Biodiversity and Conservation at the American Museum of Natural History.

3.

NOUVELLE-HOLLANDE : ILE DECRÈS.

CASOAR de la N.^{elle} Hollande. *(Casuarius novæ Hollandiæ Lath.)*

1. Casoar mâle 2. Casoar femelle 3. Jeune casoar de 5 semaines environ. Les deux individus marqués de bandes longitudinales sont âgés de 20 à 25 jours.

De l'Imprimerie de Langlois.

4.

From the Depths of the Sea:
Risso's Pioneering Studies
of Deep-Sea Life

BELLA GALIL

Author
Antoine Risso
(1777–1845)

Title
*Histoire naturelle des
principales productions du
midi de l'Europe méridionale
et particulièrment de celles
des environs de Nice et des
Alpes Maritimes*

*(Natural history of the
principal productions of
southern Europe and
particularly of those around
Nice and the Maritime Alps)*

Imprint
Paris: F.-G. Levrault, 1826

1. Left: *Stomias boa* [*Stomias
boa boa* (Risso, 1810)].* The
Scaly dragonfish is known from
depths of 1,500 meters in
the Mediterranean Sea. It has
fang-like teeth, an elongated
chin barbell—serving as a
sensory organ—and rows of
light-producing organs along
its abdomen.

A naturalist in the tradition of the eighteenth-century encyclopedists, Antoine Risso was a self-taught collector and prolific writer whose interests spanned zoology, botany, geology, paleontology, and meteorology. In our present age, when the natural sciences are segregated into ever more narrowly focused disciplines, Risso's works are a testimony to the enthusiastic spirit of the amateurs who played an important role in the revival of interest in the natural world in Europe.

Born in Nice—which was then part of the Kingdom of Sardinia—Risso was orphaned at age nine and apprenticed at fifteen to a pharmacist. Risso's early interest in botany—then still a significant part of the pharmacopeia—blossomed into a passion. At twenty-four, he was placed in charge of a local botanical garden. At the start of the Napoleonic Wars at the turn of the nineteenth century, Risso was assigned to the military hospital in his hometown, thus exempting him from the draft. The maelstrom that engulfed Europe did not deter him from pursuing his vocation. In 1810, Risso published his first volume, *Ichtyologie, ou Histoire naturelle des poissons des Alpes Maritimes*. More publications followed in quick succession, followed by a trip to Paris. On his return to Nice, Risso was nominated professor of physical and natural sciences at the Lycée Impérial.

A keen observer of nature and a resourceful collector—yet lacking access to comparative collections and scientific libraries—Risso's topically wide-ranging publications were severely criticized by his contemporaries who thought him a prolific writer of little scientific expertise: "Risso's writings embraced almost all branches of natural history without dealing with any of them in a competent way."[1] Deeply wounded by the censure of the "*savants de la capitale*," Risso wrote late in life of describing the great number of living beings with which the Creator had embellished his land, of having to rely on his observations alone, with only a copy of Carl Linnaeus's *Systema naturae* at hand, handicapped by lack of access to collection or library, and ignorant of the works at the forefront of science. But history would have the last word.

Reflecting on Risso's works on the marine life off Nice, one is impressed by the wealth of new taxa described that are fundamental to the study of the Mediterranean biota—the flora and fauna of the region. His achievements are all the more impressive when one considers that this formed but a small part of his zoological studies—themselves a small part of his life oeuvre. At the time, he was a professor of medical botany and chemistry at the École Préparatoire de Médecine et de Pharmacie of Nice, co-founder of the Philharmonic Society, and a member of the municipal council.

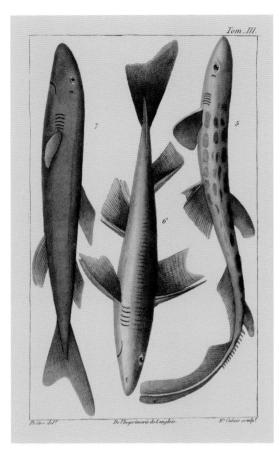

2. Center: *Acanthias Blainvillii* [*Squalus blainville* (Risso, 1827)].* Left: *Scymnus rostratus* [*Somniosus rostratus* (Risso, 1827)].* Both deepwater sharks first described by Risso, the longnose spurdog (*S. blainville*) and the little sleeper shark (*S. rostratus*)) are found in the Mediterranean Sea and north-eastern Atlantic Ocean on the continental shelf and slope.

3. *Peneus foliaceus* [*Aristaeomorpha foliacea* (Risso, 1827)].* The giant red shrimp (*A. foliacea*) is considered one of the most valuable species exploited by the deep-sea fishery in the Mediterranean Sea, although its biological characteristics indicate a high vulnerability to trawling pressure.

4. Center: *Chrysoma mediterranea* [*Scyllarus arctus* (Linnaeus, 1758)].* Under the name *C. mediterranea* (Risso, 1827), Risso described and figured the phyllosoma larva of *Scyllarus arctus,* a Mediterranean and eastern Atlantic slipper lobster that has a remarkably thin, flat, and transparent body and lives in plankton before metamorphosing into adult form.

5. Bottom center: *Squilla eusebia* [*Platysquilla eusebia* (Risso, 1816)].* The mantis shrimp *Platysquilla eusebia* is found in the Mediterranean Sea and northeastern Atlantic Ocean. It spears its prey with toothed raptorial claws.

Risso's avid curiosity led him to examine both catch and discards obtained by the local deepwater fishermen. He described crustaceans and fish collected in waters of depths up to about 3,280 feet, among them the lovingly illustrated *Aristaeomorpha foliacea* from his *Histoire naturelle* (see figure 3). Yet, the scientific community chose to embrace the fallacious "Azoic hypothesis" proposed by the British naturalist and geologist Edward Forbes, who claimed no life existed at depths greater than 300 fathoms, even when Risso's findings clearly discredited it. Nonetheless, taxonomy is a discipline with a long memory and one that honors those who were proven right, and many deep-sea species in the Mediterranean correctly bear Risso's name to this day.

The American Museum of Natural History's copy of Risso's *Histoire naturelle* was part of a famous collection assembled by Dr. John Clarkson Jay (1808–1891), the New York physician and amateur malacologist (one who studies mollusks). The American Museum of Natural History's annual report for 1874 relates the donation of "a collection of shells numbering 50,000 specimens, and a valuable library of rare conchological and scientific works, of about one thousand volumes, both formed by Dr. John C. Jay, of Rye." This major bequest—made only five years after the museum's founding and known as the "Wolfe Memorial Gift"—was made by Miss Catharine L. Wolfe, the first woman trustee of the museum and the daughter of John David Wolfe, the museum's first president.

* Risso's name followed by the current scientific name [in square brackets].

1. Bourguignat, 1861

Bella Galil is a research associate in the Division of Invertebrate Zoology at the American Museum of Natural History and a senior scientist at the National Institute of Oceanography in Haifa, Israel.

3.

Tom. V.

5

6

7

Prêtre delin.̯   De l'Imprimerie de Langlois.   V. Plée fils sculp.̯

4.

Tom. V.

8

9

10   12   11

Prêtre delin.̯   De l'Imprimerie de Langlois.   V. Plée fils sculp.̯

5.

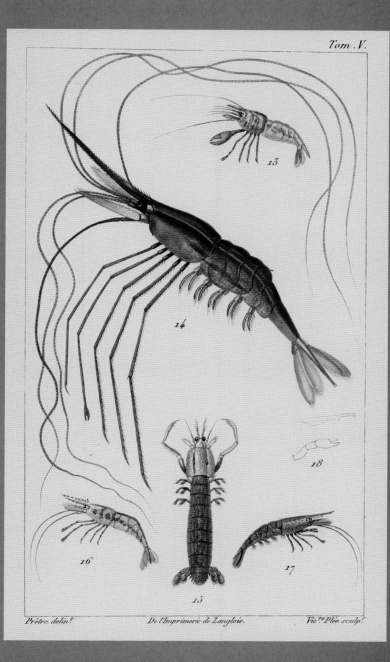

Tom. V.

13

14

18

15

16   17

Prêtre delin.̯   De l'Imprimerie de Langlois.   Vic.ᵗᵉ Plée sculp.̯

Lorenz Oken and His Magical Numerology Tour

GEORGE F. BARROWCLOUGH

Author

Lorenz Oken
(1779–1851)

Title

*Allgemeine Naturgeschichte
für alle Stände*

*(A general natural history
for everyone)*

Imprint

Stuttgart: Hoffmann,
1833–1843

1. Here Oken is illustrating variation in egg color and markings found among water birds. For example, the two large white eggs are from the two species of European storks, the two blue eggs from large European herons, and the speckled eggs from a variety of shorebirds.

Lorenz Oken was born and raised on a poor farm in Bavaria, but eventually became one of the best-known zoologists of the first half of the nineteenth century, the intellectual colleague of Johann Wolfgang von Goethe and Georges Cuvier. Oken held major academic posts in Germany and Switzerland; founded, edited, and published a highly influential journal; and wrote many books, including one on the art of war. In addition to his popular works, he is best known for his general theories attempting to provide an understanding of the laws of physics, chemistry, and nature.

At the dawn of the nineteenth century, scientific theories were considered essentially a branch of philosophy and not constrained by experiment. In his early twenties, Oken became a proponent of the then ascendant Naturphilosophie school of thought, based on ideas taken from the well-known German philosopher Immanuel Kant. Oken could classify things according to any organizing principle that made sense to him. He could also, and did, propose theories about ontogeny; the cellular organization of life; the nature of light, color, and heat; and the natural system of minerals. He speculated about the nature and organization of anything and everything in the universe. Unfortunately, in the absence of an evolutionary world view or experimental evidence, the organizing principle of the day often was numerology, and, in the case of natural philosophers, this was a fascination with threes and fives. Oken published an influential treatise arguing that all of life—indeed, all of nature, including rocks and minerals—could be organized along a natural scale reflecting the sophistication of the five sensory systems. For example, fish have a tongue, hence taste; lizards have a nose, thus smell; birds have an external ear opening and can hear; and mammals, in addition to all of the above, possess movable eyes with two lids—fully developed sight. This "intrinsic" structure sometimes resulted in awkward alliances of species now known to have nothing to do with each other. Still, the structure provided a great basis for organization, and Oken used it as the organizing principle for his multivolume illustrated guide to natural history.

Oken's magnificent *Allgemeine Naturgeschichte für alle Stände*—a natural history written for all readers—ranged in content from geology (including fossils) to plants and animals, and included very detailed illustrations of human anatomy. Published between 1833 and 1843 in a series of thirteen volumes of text, plus an additional volume of plates, the widely distributed guide was a kind of popular encyclopedia of nature, useful for teaching or general reference. The illustrations consisted of engravings and lithographs by Johann Susemihl. The twenty-nine lithographic plates of birds, their nests, and eggs were individually hand colored. They include birds from all over the world, many of which, given the time, neither Oken

97

2. Miscellaneous eggs, mostly of songbirds, and two interesting nests. The nests of the long-tailed tit (upper) and penduline tit (lower) are both woven from plant material and may take the birds several weeks to complete. The domed top effectively conceals the eggs from predators. For small birds with uncovered nests, speckling on the eggs may act as disruptive camouflage.

3. Six waterfowl (*Wasserhühner*) from around the world. Although none of these is a traditional waterfowl (e.g., ducks, geese, and swans), all are associated with aquatic habitats. The jacana (middle left) is an example of a polyandrous species in which females have multiple mates and the males build the nests, incubate the eggs, and take care of the young.

4. Oken labeled this plate "*Trappen*," or bustards, after the great bustard of Europe (middle left). But, in fact, the other species illustrated here are now known to be unrelated to bustards. The dodo (upper left) provided food for many a hungry sailor in the Indian Ocean before being driven to extinction; it was actually a large flightless pigeon.

5. Six unrelated marsh birds (*Sumpfvögel*). Although only three of these occur in Europe, the illustrations are all reasonably accurate, capturing idiosyncrasies of the neck, legs, and bill of each. The long legs allow these water birds to wade; the bills are adapted to their diverse feeding habits.

nor Susemihl could have been personally familiar with. Rather, most of the illustrations were copied from plates previously published in other books.

Oken's natural history might seem quirky and esoteric to the modern natural history enthusiast. Almost as many plates are devoted to eggs as to the birds themselves, but this reflects a long fascination amateur naturalists have had with egg collecting. Before the availability of inexpensive, quality binoculars, bird-watching was not a widely popular pastime, and many students of natural history probably were egg collectors (oologists) apt to be enthralled with the diversity of egg color, shape, size, and markings. Today, it is illegal for private citizens to have an egg or nest collection, and, among professional ornithologists, more attention is generally paid to birds' nests than their eggs. This reflects our current interest in birds' decisions about nest placement and nest concealment, and in the evolution of elaborate nest architecture. For example, in the plate illustrated above, the side entrance of the carefully woven nest of a long-tailed tit keeps the eggs concealed from potential predators, such as jays and hawks.

Oken contributed some substantive observations on vertebrate ontogeny that are still appreciated by modern workers. However, the numerology of the natural philosophers fell to the advances of experimental science during the latter half of the nineteenth century. *Allgemeine Naturgeschichte für alle Stände* has been superseded by modern field guides and natural history handbooks, but the volumes are still studied by science historians. Today, it is one of the iconic works sought by rare book dealers and bibliophiles, and is one of the treasured natural history books of the nineteenth century.

George F. Barrowclough *is an associate curator in the Ornithology Department in the Division of Vertebrate Zoology at the American Museum of Natural History.*

3.

4.

5.

Drawn by R. Hills Esq. Engraved by J. Zeitter.

Camelopardalis Giraffa.

Art in the Service of Science

NINA J. ROOT

Title
Proceedings of the Zoological Society of London

Imprint
London: The Society,
1833–1965

Title
Transactions of the Zoological Society of London

Imprint
London: The Society,
1835–1984

1. A newborn giraffe
(*Camelopardis giraffa*) and
mother at the London Zoo.
Artist Robert Hills (1769–
1841) was the founder of the
Society of Painters in Watercolour. This is the only illustration
he did for the *Zoological Society
Transactions and Proceedings*.

The journals *Proceedings of the Zoological Society of London* and *Transactions of the Zoological Society of London* were important disseminators of information about previously unknown, often exotic species discovered around the world. The eighteenth and nineteenth centuries were times of great exploring expeditions that identified many new species and returned home with live and preserved specimens to the delight of a curious European public and natural scientists anxious to learn about these "new" creatures.

When visiting Paris, Sir Thomas Standford Raffles, the British statesman and a product of Britain's far-flung colonies, was impressed by the Jardin des Plantes and its impressive zoo, many of whose inhabitants were imported from the French colonies and holdings. He wondered why England didn't have a similar institution to study and exhibit the faunal diversity and resources of the British Empire. Raffles and Sir Humphry Davy, president of the Royal Society, organized the Zoological Society of London in 1826, to "introduce new varieties, breeds, or races of living animals . . . which may be judged capable of application to purposes of utility, either in farm yards, woods, wastes, ponds, or rivers, and to establish a general zoological collection, consisting of prepared specimens in the different classes and orders, so as to afford a view of the animal kingdom at large." Although not stated in the objectives, it was generally known that Raffles envisioned that a zoological garden would be established. At the Zoological Society's first general meeting on April 29, 1826, the objectives were amended to "the formation of a Collection of Living Animals; a museum of preserved animals; and a library connected with the subject." The following year, ladies were admitted as members, a first for scientific societies—since the study of nature was considered an acceptable interest for women. Intelligence tests were waived for ladies' memberships. "Ladies" were not encouraged to attend meetings, because Victorian modesty proscribed any mention of anatomy, limbs, reproduction, or sexual organs in their presence.

Regular meetings were held to report the latest zoological findings and discoveries. To avoid clashing with scriptural creation theology of the time, speculative theories were avoided, and only descriptive reports of newly discovered or cataloged species were read. Corresponding members from all parts of the British Empire, Europe, and America were encouraged to submit reports of new species. To widely disseminate the scientific reports, the *Proceedings of the Zoological Society of London* was first published in 1833, and in 1835 the *Transactions of the Zoological Society of London* was established to publish in-depth articles. The two periodicals became important sources where scientific discoveries and research were published. The foremost scientists of the day presented papers at the society's meetings,

J G Keulemans lith.   Hanhart imp.

1.   COLIUS NIGRICOLLIS
2. 3. COLIUS ERYTHROMELON

2.

2. Colys, or African mouse birds, by John Gerrard Keulemans. A Dutch artist, Keulemans moved to England, where he illustrated bird books. The birds are brightly and accurately depicted.

3. The head of a Somali gazelle (*Amadorcas clarkei*) shown one-third its natural size. Joseph Smit (1836–1929) painted and lithographed the illustration. Smit was considered the best animal artist in England after Wolf's death.

4. The bat hawk (*Macheirhanphus alcinus*) has a wide range: from sub-Saharan Africa and South Asia to New Guinea. Joseph Wolf (1820–1899), considered the finest nineteenth-century bird artist, included in the illustration details of the hawk's eye, bill, and claw.

5. The young hippopotamus Obayasch (1849–1878) in the Cairo garden of the British Consulate, awaiting transport to the London Zoo. The consul, Mr. Murray, described the hippo as being as playful as a Newfoundland puppy. Joseph Wolf, the Zoological Society's principal artist, painted the charming youngster from a sketch.

describing recent additions to the zoo, newly discovered species, and anatomical findings. Such notables as Sir Richard Owens, H. Godwin-Austen, John Gould, Prince Lucien Bonaparte, P. L. Sclater, and Walter Rothschild were among the contributors.

In 1848, the *Proceedings* began to illustrate its scientific reports with visual descriptions to support the naturalists' papers. (*Transactions* had been illustrated since its inception in 1835.) Scientists sought the best artists to illustrate their articles, and as the nineteenth century produced some of the greatest natural history artists, there were many from which to choose: Joseph Wolf, considered by many to be the finest bird illustrator of the century; Edward Lear of nonsense verse fame; Joseph Smit; John Keulemans; Elizabeth Gould; and Henrik Gronvold are but a few of the fine artists who contributed to the publications. The zoo provided the models for many of the illustrations.

The *Proceedings* was absorbed by the *Journal of Zoology* in 1965, as was *Transactions* in 1984. With the advent of photography, artistic illustrations were supplanted by photographic images. The scientific descriptions of species, including many first diagnoses of unknown animals, remain important to science to this day, and the prolific natural history art that enhanced these descriptions is still admired for its beauty and scientific importance.

Nina J. Root is the Director Emerita of the Research Library at the American Museum of Natural History.

3.

P Z.S.1891 Pl.XXI

J.Smit del et lith.   ⅓   Mintern Bros. imp.

AMMODORCAS CLARKEI.

4.

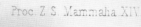

Trans.Zool.Soc.Vol.6 Pl.29.

J.Wolf del.et lith.   MACHEIRHAMPHUS ALCINUS.   M.& N.Hanhart imp.

5.

Proc.Z.S.Mammalia.XIV

Wolf lith. From a Sketch made at Cairo. Dec.1849.   Printed by Hullmandel & Walton.

YOUNG HIPPOPOTAMUS
Presented to the Zoological Society by H.H.Abbas Pasha.

1.

3.

2.

Prêtre pinx. Borromée dir. Héna sc.

The First Comprehensive Description of the Amphibians and Reptiles of the World

CHRISTOPHER J. RAXWORTHY

Author

André-Marie-Constant
Duméril (1774–1860),
Gabriel Bibron (1806–1848),
and Auguste Henri André
Duméril (1812–1870)

Title

Erpétologie générale, ou
histoire naturelle complète
des reptiles

(General herpetology, or
complete natural history
of reptiles)

Imprint

Paris: Roret, 1834–1854

1. Figure 1 is the *Furcifer
verrucosus* (Madagascar warty
chameleon). The swollen tail
base and elevated rear of the
head identify this as an adult
male. Figure 2 shows the
tongue of *Chamaeleo
senegalensis* (Senegal
chameleon). Many chameleons
can extend the tongue to twice
their body length. Figure 3 is
the dorsal head view of a male
Furcifer bifidus (two-horned
Madagascar chameleon). The
function of these horns, which
are absent in females, is still
poorly known.

At the start of the eighteenth century, there was only a rudimentary understanding of the global diversity of amphibians and reptiles. Yet, for the Muséum National d'Histoire Naturelle, this was a time of massive growth of its herpetological collections, as specimens from all over the world were being amassed as a result of France's economic and military power. During this period, André-Marie-Constant Duméril, a professor of ichthyology and herpetology at the Paris museum, became responsible for curating the largest and most diverse herpetological collection in the world.

A physician and anatomist by training, Duméril was nominated by George Cuvier in 1803 to replace Count de Lacepède as the head of ichthyology and herpetology at the museum. A.-M.-C. Duméril's research interests centered on developing a revised higher-level taxonomic organization for all genera of amphibians and reptiles, as well as detailed descriptions of the many new species that were being discovered. For this enormous latter task, Duméril was aided by his chief assistant, Gabriel Bibron, who carefully examined and described much of the museum's collection between 1832 and 1848. In 1834, they published the first volume of the *Erpétologie générale*, with the ultimate goal of providing the first comprehensive scientific account of the amphibians and reptiles of the world.

The *Erpétologie générale, ou histoire naturelle complète des reptiles* was published over a period of twenty years, between 1834 and 1854, as a nine-volume set (with Volume 7 in two parts) and an 1854 atlas of plates. The series included detailed descriptions of 1,393 species with 108 beautifully drawn plates (not 120 as stated on the atlas's title page). The hand-painted color plates are remarkable for their life-like poses of dead and sometimes poorly preserved museum specimens. Their depictions required considerable skill from the artists and authors, as well as some guesswork, especially concerning coloration in life, which was impossible to preserve after death. Many new species were described in these volumes, and complete bibliographies and summaries of the biology of each group were also provided.

The entire work projects a strong feeling of great confidence, authority, and understanding from the authors; reading this today, you still get the impression that this catalog is comprehensive and complete. Sadly, Gabriel Bibron died prematurely of tuberculosis in 1848, before the series was completed, which led to a hiatus in publication. However, Auguste Henri André Duméril, the son of A.-M.-C. Duméril, completed Bibron's work for Volumes 7 and 9 and the atlas. Inevitably, over the course of twenty years, the earlier volumes became incomplete, as a large quantity of new specimens continued to be cataloged in Paris and new species described. Yet, interestingly, the authors chose not to update or supplement these earlier volumes

Reptiles.   Pl. 92.

1 Dactylethre du Cap. 1a. Sa bouche ouverte. 2. Tête de Pipa vue en dessus. 2 a. Une de ses pattes de devant.
2 b. Une de ses pattes postérieures.

2.

2. At top is the *Xenopus laevis* (African-clawed frog). This completely aquatic frog was bred in large numbers in the laboratory for human pregnancy testing. The claws can be used to rake prey and aid in scavenging. At bottom left is the *Pipa pipa* (Surinam, or star-fingered, toad). The bizarre fingertips in this flattened frog are used to detect prey (mostly invertebrates) in river-bottom mud.

3. The *Python sebae* (African rock python) is Africa's largest snake, with specimens reported to exceed 20 feet. This species is often an ambush feeder, striking and holding its prey with its jaws and then killing it by suffocation using its powerful body muscles to constrict. Prey include rodents, monkeys, antelopes, monitor lizards, and even crocodiles.

4. At top is the *Geochelone sulcata* (African spur-thighed tortoise). The largest mainland tortoise in the world, this giant can reach more than 200 pounds in weight. Below is the *Pyxis arachnoides* (Madagascar spider tortoise), one of Madagascar's smallest tortoises. This species lives in arid costal regions and is remarkable for laying a single, large egg.

5. Pictured is the *Ptychozoon kuhli* (Flying gecko). The flaps of skin on the body, limbs, and tail, and the webbing on the hands and feet of this Southeast Asian gecko have two benefits which allow it (1) to glide, or parachute, in forest canopy, and (2) to blend into tree bark to avoid being detected by predators such as birds.

Christopher J. Raxworthy is the Associate Dean of Science for Education and Exhibition and an associate curator in the Herpetology Department in the Division of Vertebrate Zoology at the American Museum of Natural History.

within the *Erpétologie générale*, perhaps in recognition of the ever-expanding species diversity and of A.-M.-C. Duméril's primary interest in the higher-level taxonomic organization of amphibians and reptiles.

It is difficult to overemphasize the importance of the *Erpétologie générale* to the field of herpetology. This series set a standard for herpetological reference, with copies deposited in many of the major scientific libraries of the period, and because of the accuracy of the species descriptions, it continues to be widely used and cited today. However, the taxonomic organization that A.-M.-C. Duméril used is now considered completely unconventional by today's scientific community. For instance, in the *Erpétologie générale*, amphibians are treated as one of the four orders within Reptilia, along with turtles, snakes, and lizards (which also included crocodiles).

Our volumes were gifted to the American Museum of Natural History in 1922 from the library of Robert L. Stuart, a founder of the museum and its second president. Due to the academic utility and longevity of the *Erpétologie générale*, the museum library has bound the atlas volume's plates into each volume in order to aid in their practical use by researchers. And as a testament to the ongoing significance of these volumes in the early twenty-first century, complete digital versions have recently become available online at the Biodiversity Heritage Library—of which the American Museum of Natural History is a founding member—and almost half of the museum library's volumes were on loan to staff herpetologists at the time of writing this article. Together, these rare, original library copies—and digital versions—will ensure that the *Erpétologie générale* continues to exist as a vibrant living contribution to the study of herpetology.

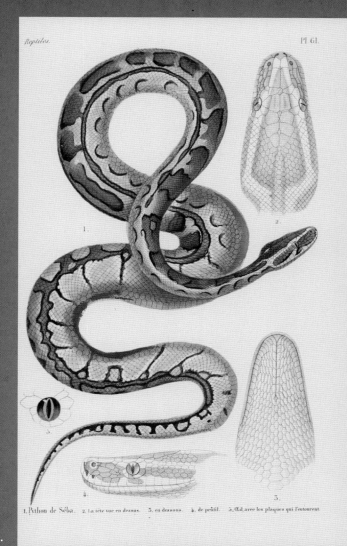

1. Python de Séba. 2. La tête vue en dessus. 3. en dessous. 4. de profil. 5. Œil avec les plaques qui l'entourent.

3.

Pretre pinx.　　　　　　Borromee dir.　　　　　Davesne sc.

1. Tortue sillonnée. *Testudo sulcata.* N.º 7, pag. 74, 2.ª Volume.
1 a. son Sternum.
2. Pyxide arachnoïde. *Pyxis arachnoïdes.* N.º 1, pag. 156, 2.ª Vol.
2 a. la même vue en dessous.

4.

Pretre del.　　　　　　　　　　　　Barrois sc.

1. Platydactyle Homalocéphale. *Tome III, pag. 339. N.º 17.* 1 a. Extrémité du tronc et origine de la queue en dessous.

5.

NORTHERN CIRCUMPOLAR MAP
for each Month in the Year.

Scale of Magnitudes

2 3 4 5 6 7 Neb.

Engraved by W. G. Evans New York, under the Direction of E. H. Burritt.

Hartford, Published by F. J. HUNTINGTON 1835, Entered according to act of Congress Sept. 1st 1832 by F. J. Huntington, of the State of Connecticut.

Burritt's Sky Atlases

NEIL DEGRASSE TYSON

Author
Elijah H. Burritt
(1794–1838)

Title
*Atlas designed to illustrate the
geography of the heavens*

Imprint
New York: [multiple
publishers], 1835–1856

In prescientific, preliterate eras, when we were all quite sure the heavens controlled our fate, the celestial sky was a storyteller's palette. Different legends matter to each of the world's cultures, and it's these stories, illustrated by the imagination of the listener, that would create a kind of shared oral history for all our ancestors.

The romance of these centuries of sky lore remains with us today, but only as a quaint and faded reminder of our earliest attempts to understand and interpret the heavens. We have not renamed the constellations. We have not modernized the stories. We have not redrawn the boundaries. They remain for us all as ornaments on the celestial sphere—thousands of stars, tracing eighty-eight constellations, spanning the sky.

The earliest atlases of the constellations offered nothing more than the proper locations of the stars, their brightness relative to one another, and the illustrator's best attempt to bring the legends to life. In the eighteenth and nineteenth centuries, however, more and more science of the universe became available to the celestial mapmaker. Almost in recoil from this encroaching force, the illustrations became less ornate—the constellations carried less meaning—as cosmic discovery crept inward, inch by inch, first along the margins, then occupying entire pages of data on the Sun, Moon, planets, and stars. No longer would the maps issue forth solely from our imagination—they would carry a detailed record of our scientific progress as well.

The nineteenth century in particular saw the discovery of Neptune, the application of spectroscopy, the associated discovery of chemical elements in the stars, the full cataloging of non-stellar objects in the night sky, detailed observations of the Sun and its spots, and a precise understanding of the myriad orbits enjoyed by the Sun's family of planets, moons, asteroids, and comets—all a kind of cosmic ballet, choreographed by the forces of gravity.

Elijah Burritt's star volumes—in successively updated editions within the nineteenth century—would exemplify the transition from atlas-as-art to atlas-as-reference and stargazing tool. The constellation figures of the seasonal star maps are all there, in expected mythological detail. However, only in the earlier editions are they hand colored. In later editions they're left as line drawings. And in all editions they are omitted from the full-sky Mercator map projections at the book's end so that the reader sees just the stars, an outline of the Milky Way, and the celestial grid on which they've been placed. Meanwhile, whole pages are given to illustrated data on the known planets, moons, comets, and asteroids of the solar system—especially their relative sizes and distances. These spreads further offer engravings of planetary

1. A major feature of Burritt's
atlas are these celestial maps,
which illustrate visible stars and
constellation figures depicted
as gods or animals from
mythology or as contemporary
scientific instruments.

109

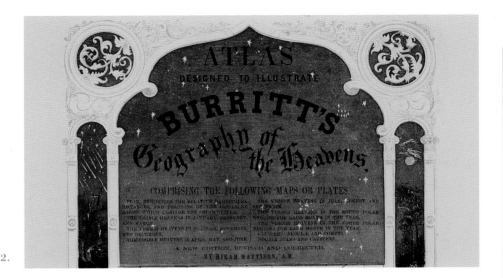

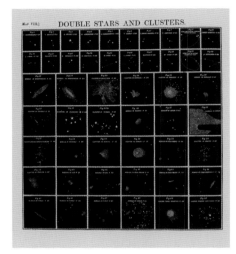

2. Burritt created his atlas as a lower-cost alternative to celestial globes, thereby encouraging the public to become directly involved in astronomy by making their own observations. Several editions of Burritt's atlas were published between 1835 and 1856, producing over 300,000 copies.

3. These charts, added to later editions of Burritt's atlas, illustrate a number of heavenly objects such as double stars, star clusters, nebulae, and comets, including the Comet of 1689, the Comet of 1744, the Great Comet of 1680, the Great Comet of 1811, Halley's Comet, the Great Comet of 1819, and the Comet of 1843.

4. William Herschel discovered Uranus in 1781, calling it "the Georgium Sidus" for George III of England. Americans, including Burritt, referred to the planet by its discoverer's name. Astronomer Johann Elert Bode proposed the name change to "Uranus" for the ancient Greek deity of the heavens, but this name didn't come into common use until about 1850.

5. In 1856, publisher Henry Whitall adapted Burritt's map to produce a planisphere, essentially a flattened version of the astrolabe, showing the position of the heavens at any given time for latitude 40 degrees north (this included Philadelphia, Denver, and San Francisco).

Neil deGrasse Tyson is an astrophysicist and the Frederick Priest Rose Director of the Hayden Planetarium at the American Museum of Natural History.

and cometary orbits around the Sun, captured with an almost boastful level of detail and precision.

Given the recent flap over Pluto's demotion from planet status, one can't help notice Burritt's list of planets that appears in his 1830s editions. They include four that had been recently discovered: Ceres, Pallas, Vesta, and Juno. By the 1850s, however, after dozens more planets were found orbiting the Sun in a shared region of space, these would all be reclassified as asteroids—a newly invented category at the time. Such was the pace of discovery at the time—a kind of joyous nightmare for the publisher of an atlas whose mission included bringing the frontier of cosmic discovery to the reader. Of course, in an earlier era, an atlas of just the millennia-old legends of the night sky would have required no updates at all.

In the latest editions of Burritt's atlas, you can even find thumbnail illustrations of double stars, star clusters, nebulae, and other fun objects to observe in the night sky. Coming full swing, twentieth-century star atlases hardly portray the constellations at all. They're mostly unadorned stick figures. Yes, the official boundaries are indicated, but these books are primarily primers for stargazers, complete with listings of objects that make excellent targets for backyard telescopes—just as Elijah H. Burritt surely had envisioned what the future of the celestial atlases would be.

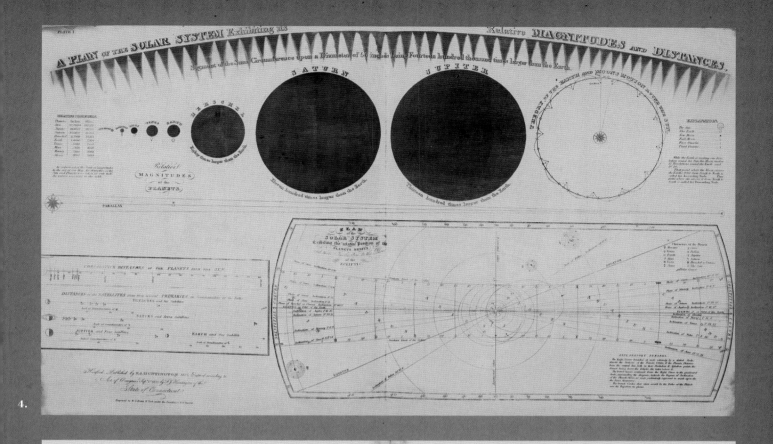

4.

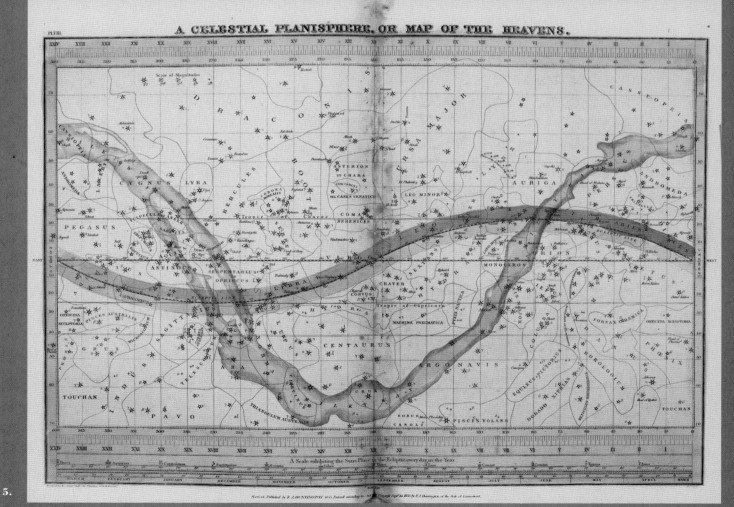

5.

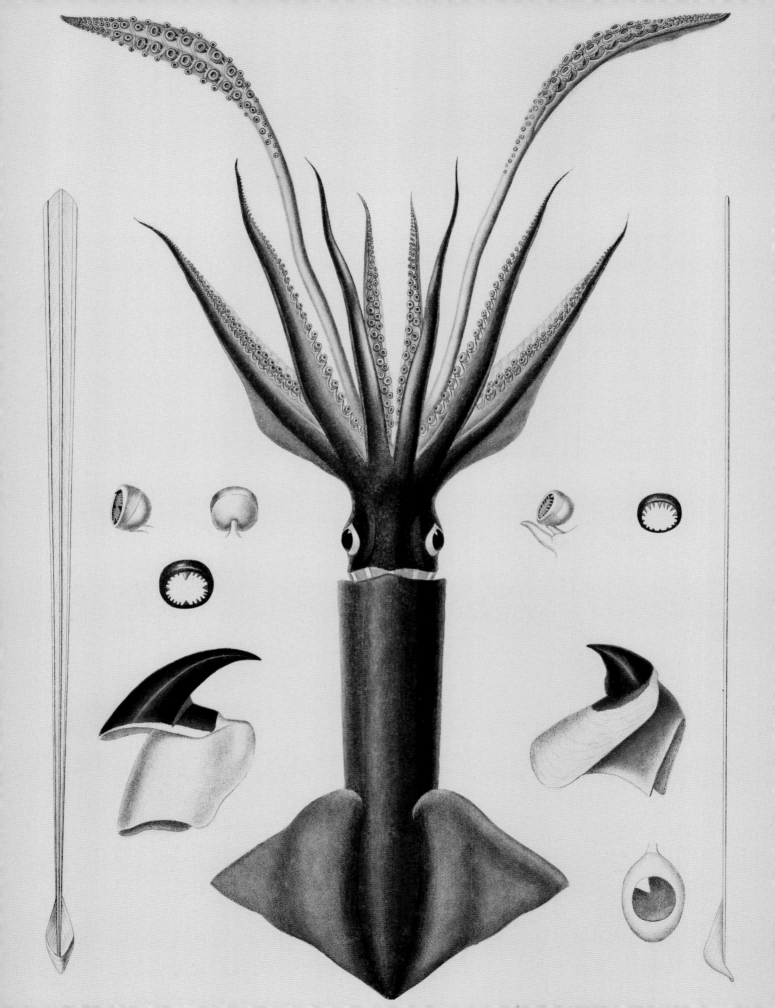

Alcide d'Orbigny:
Darwin's Rival Naturalist

NILES ELDREDGE

Author
Alcide Dessalines d'Orbigny
(1802–1857)

Title
*Voyage dans l'Amérique
méridionale: le Brésil, la
République Orientale de
l'Uruguay, la République
Argentine, la Patagonie,
la République du Chili, la
République de Bolivia, la
République du Pérou, exécuté
pendant les années 1826,
1827, 1828, 1829, 1830,
1831, 1832, et 1833*

*(Voyage in South America:
Brazil, the Oriental Republic
of Uruguay, the Argentine
Republic, Patagonia, the
Republic of Chile, the Republic
of Bolivia, the Republic of
Peru, made during the years
1826, 1827, 1828, 1829,
1830, 1831, 1832, and 1833)*

Imprint
Paris: Pitois-Levrault,
Strasbourg, Ve. Levrault,
1835–1847

1. *Loligo gigas*, now called
Dosidcus gigas—and known
as the Humboldt squid—is
an aggressive and carnivorous
nocturnal predator that inhabits
the eastern Pacific. D'Orbigny
reported seeing massive die-offs
of this large species along
hundreds of miles of the
Chilean coast.

The great naturalist explorer, geologist, and paleontologist Alcide Dessalines d'Orbigny was born in France in 1802. He is best remembered as a paleontologist who pioneered the study of microscopic fossils for recognizing divisions of geological time and for his later monumental works on French paleontology. He is often seen as the father of micropaleontology, who originally named the important group of tiny, shelled amoebas known as foraminiferans.

However, less well known is d'Orbigny's exploits as a superb general naturalist. His classic explorations of southern South America over a six-year span preceded Darwin's better-known South American exploration on H.M.S. *Beagle* (1832–1835) by some six years. Visiting Brazil, Uruguay, Argentina, Chile, Bolivia, and Peru between the years 1826 and 1833, d'Orbigny made important observations on the anthropology, zoology, botany, and paleontology of South America and amassed huge collections of insects, birds, mammals, reptiles, amphibians, fishes, plants, and non-insect terrestrial—as well as marine—invertebrates. He collected fossils, his primary lifelong passion, and made geographic and geological observations. The grand total of his collections of living organisms alone is said to have included more than 9,000 species, of which many were new to science.

On his return home, d'Orbigny turned to the important task of publishing the scientific results of his arduous, yet productive, South American expedition. Between 1835 and 1847, d'Orbigny published eleven discipline-specific volumes, totaling some 4,747 pages illustrated with 555 lithographic plates. Together, these volumes comprise his work *Voyage dans l'Amérique méridionale (Voyage in South America)*.

Not long after returning home, he was hard at work on a study of French rocks and fossils, parallel works on molluscan fossils and stratigraphic zonation of the world, in addition to other works outlining his theoretical conclusions, which were no less monumental in scope. But it was the relationship d'Orbigny held—from a distance—with Charles Darwin that accounts for one of the greatest, albeit seldom recognized, contributions d'Orbigny made to scientific history.

At the outset of Darwin's experiences as a fledgling naturalist in South America, he was all too keenly aware of the presence of d'Orbigny, a seasoned veteran still in South America. Twice (in 1832 and again in 1835) Darwin wrote to his mentor, John Stevens Henslow, and expressed his anxiety that d'Orbigny would be the early bird that got all the delicious worms. And, indeed, it was inevitable that such would be the case. The most ironic is that the bird still sometimes called "Darwin's rhea" —which was extremely important to Darwin's early evolutionary thinking—was, in fact, first discovered and named by d'Orbigny. Darwin was both inspired by, and competitive with, his predecessor and rival.

And, it is fair to say that in many ways d'Orbigny may well have been the superior naturalist. By the 1840s, while both men were busy writing up their results, Darwin seemed to accede to d'Orbigny's opinion, especially on matters involving the fossil record. Darwin would later call d'Orbigny's series of monographs and plates on South American natural history one of the monuments of nineteenth-century science. Yet, of course, it was Darwin who came back from South America with a theory on evolution.

Was d'Orbigny just a describer of nature and not a theorist? Not at all. D'Orbigny died just two years before Darwin published *On the Origin of Species* in 1859. He never was an evolutionist, because his mentor was the famous paleontologist and father of Comparative Anatomy, Georges Cuvier. Cuvier was no evolutionist but a "catastrophist," who thought that extinction of entire faunas in the geological past came before separate creations of entire new species.

After his return from South America, d'Orbigny's work on the geological distributions of fossils showed a series of what he called "stages"—divisions of rocks defined by discrete assemblages of fossils. Most seemed to become extinct at about the same time and then replaced by newly appearing species that defined the succeeding stage. D'Orbigny thought his stages were worldwide in extent and published these thoughts, which aligned with views Cuvier had published thirty years earlier. In the interim, however, geologists had moved away from such catastrophist theories. The current literature at the time, with which Darwin was familiar, contained no support for Cuvier's ideas on catastrophic extinction and subsequent creation of new faunas.

Yet, in a footnote to an early 1844 *Essay* on evolution not published in Darwin's lifetime, Darwin wrote, "If species really, after catastrophes, created in showers over world, my theory false." It is likely that the source of Darwin's last-minute angst was caused by his old rival and nemesis, Alcide d'Orbigny. D'Orbigny had, in effect, resurrected Cuvier's ideas of "revolutions" of life over the surface of the globe when he introduced his concept of geological stages that he thought were a global phenomenon. Darwin's theory was not false, of course, but neither was d'Orbigny's. His stages, although not universally distributed "the world over," are nonetheless empirically valid and still in use today. Both scientists were right, and the resolution of Darwinian evolution with d'Orbigny's stages is only now being achieved in evolutionary biology.

2. Now called *Potamotrygon hystrix,* the porcupine stingray is a freshwater fish. The barb at the end of its tail is very poisonous. Indians use these as arrow-points and "fear the fish more than pirhana."

3. D'Orbigny saved the mammal section of the book for last, but other work overwhelmed him and the mammal descriptions were very brief. The black-capped squirrel monkey seen here is found in Bolivia, where it lives in large groups and subsists mainly on arthropods.

4. D'Orbigny noted that these freshwater snails, now known as *Pomacea canaliculata,* have highly variable shells. Found in Argentina and Bolivia, these mollusks are considered highly invasive species in Asia, where they were imported as a food item.

5. D'Orbigny describes at length his observations of a single octopus, how it hid in a rock, caught small fish that swam by, and crawled painfully on dry rocks. D'Orbigny had the mollusk seize him with its tentacles and remarked that it took great force to get rid of it due to its strong suction cups.

Niles Eldredge is a curator emeritus in the Division of Paleontology at the American Museum of Natural History.

2.

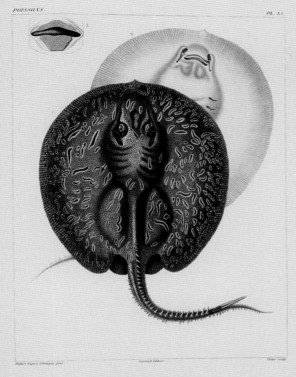

POISSONS.

Pl. 15.

1-3. TRYGON histrix. *Müll. Henl.*

3.

MAMMIFÈRES.

Pl. 4.

CALITRIX entomophagus. *d'Orb.*

4.

MOLLUSQUES.

1-5. AMPULLARIA scalaris. 1-4. A. canaliculata.
5-6. A. canaliculata.

5.

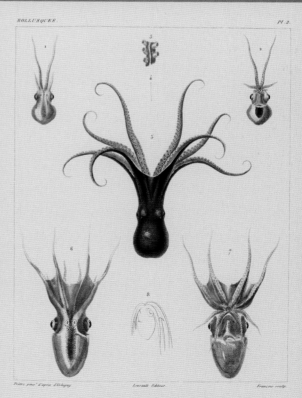

MOLLUSQUES.

Pl. 2.

1-4. OCTOPUS atlanticus, *d'Orb.* 5. O. fontanianus, *d'Orb.*
6-8. O. quoyanus, *d'Orb.*

MON-CHONSIA.

A KANSAS CHIEF.

PUBLISHED BY DANIEL RICE & JAMES G. CLARK, PHILADA.

Drawn, Printed & Cold at the Lithographic & Print Colouring Establishmen. 94 Walnut St Phila

Entered according to act of Congress in the Year 1842 by James G. Clark in the Clerks office of the District Court of the Eastern District of Pa.

Colonel McKenney's Indian Gallery

PETER M. WHITELEY

Author
Thomas L. McKenney
(1785–1859) and James Hall
(1793–1868)

Title
*History of the Indian tribes
of North America, with
biographical sketches and
anecdotes of the principal
chiefs; embellished with one
hundred and twenty portraits
from the Indian Gallery in
the Department of War at
Washington*

Imprint
Philadelphia: E. C. Biddle,
1837–1844

The fruit of more than twenty years' labor, these volumes were the brainchild of Thomas L. McKenney, a flamboyant, larger-than-life character, who served as the Superintendent of Indian Trade from 1816 to 1822 and as the first Commissioner of Indian Affairs from 1824 to 1830. Upon assuming office in 1816, McKenney began to assemble an "Indian Archive," or museum, at his base in the War Department. Its centerpiece would be a portrait gallery depicting all Native American delegations visiting the nation's capital. In 1822, he had the great good luck to enlist Charles Bird King, the renowned artist and student of Benjamin West, as principal portraitist. By 1830, more than one hundred images had been completed, the earliest collection of genuine portraits of Native Americans as named and known individuals. The "Indian Gallery" hung on a wall in McKenney's offices in Georgetown.

Delighted with King's works, McKenney soon sought to publish the gallery, via the relatively new invention of lithography. He attracted much initial interest among subscribers, who quickly saw the national importance of the project; indeed, John Quincy Adams agreed to be editor (uncredited) on the historical narrative included in the first volume. But McKenney quickly fell afoul of President Andrew Jackson, who saw Indians only as an obstacle to American expansion, and he was fired from office in 1830.

Anxious to retain access to the archive, McKenney arranged to have the paintings copied over the next several years by New York artist Henry Inman. It was from Inman's copies that the lithographs were made, and, after a series of trials and tribulations, the first volume was finally published in 1837, with an accompanying text authored largely by James Hall, McKenney's newly acquired partner. The text contains many valuable vignettes, but is typically anecdotal, secondhand, and firmly within the "savagist" tradition of nineteenth-century representations of Native American life—the McKenney/Adams history is the much better textual component.

As for the pictures, that is another matter. King's paintings became justly famous and were accounted a national treasure. The vibrant lithographic translations astonished a fascinated public and are still a jewel to behold today. Each image from the engraver's stone was hand colored by a team of watercolorists (with significant variations among copies). Many historic figures are depicted, both from life and in a few cases from other pictures copied mostly by King. Included, among many others, are: Sequoyah (Cherokee, figure 2); Red Jacket (Seneca); Thayendanegea, or Joseph Brant (Mohawk); Black Hawk (Sauk, figure 3); Wanata ("Grand Chief of the Sioux"); and Osceola (Seminole).

Eventually, the original paintings were transferred to the Smithsonian Institution, where they were exhibited from 1858 to 1865. Tragically, all were lost

1. Monchonsia, or
White Plume (Kansa).

117

2.

2. Sequoyah (Cherokee).

3. Black Hawk (Sauk).

4. Sharitarish (Pawnee).

5. Hayne Hudjihini, or Female Eagle (Oto). The museum's oil painting is shown here side by side with the published lithograph.

in the Smithsonian fire of 1865. (Inman's copies survive at the Peabody Museum at Harvard.) In some cases, fortunately, King had painted additional images, which survive in various collections, including some at the White House. The published volumes remain the major record of McKenney's Indian Gallery, with a few exceptions. One intriguing exception involves the American Museum of Natural History's library: six small oil paintings depict the same individuals whose portraits launched King's involvement with the project. Attributed either to King or to Samuel Seymour, neither was likely the true artist, whose identity remains unknown. Less polished than the King paintings, they are nonetheless remarkably convincing. The six individuals were from an Upper Missouri delegation to Washington in 1821 to 1822, including Pawnee chiefs Petalesharro and Sharitarish (figure 4); Monchonsia, or White Plume (Kansa, figure 1); Ongpatonga, or Big Elk (Omaha); and Shaumonekusse, or Prairie Wolf (Oto). Of special interest is Shaumonekusse's young wife Hayne Hudjihini or Female Eagle (Oto, figure 5), one of the earliest real portraits of a Native American woman. (King's original is among those owned by the White House.) The museum's oil painting is shown side by side with the published lithograph.

McKenney and Hall's *History of the Indian tribes of North America* is a remarkable document. Its text may be dated, but the gorgeous, meticulous lithographs live on as a testament to a vital moment of (Native) American history and culture, to the indomitable will of Colonel McKenney, and to the consummate skill of Charles Bird King. It remains an important record and a true national treasure.

Peter M. Whiteley is a curator in the Division of Anthropology at the American Museum of Natural History.

MA-KA-TAI-ME-SHE-KIA-KIAH
OR
BLACK HAWK A SAUKE BRAVE

PUBLISHED BY F. W. GREENOUGH, PHILAD.ª

3.

SHAR-I-TAR-ISH,
A PAWNEE CHIEF.

PUBLISHED BY J. T. BOWEN, PHILAD.ª

4.

HAYNE HUDJIHINI EAGLE OF DELIGHT.

Philadelphia Published by F. W. Biddle

5.

WE re
many ha
does not
a softne
and su
of the
of a

Sh
to sa
by
sev
re
of

probably jars
the most, very deliberate
his own nose, ears, and neck. If she was
she was no doubt better pleased in administering to her
have been in gratifying her own.

Shortly after her return home she died, and the bereaved husband was so sensibly
VOL. L—21

Rhea Darwinii.

Darwin's Voyage of Discovery

NANCY B. SIMMONS

Editor

Charles Darwin
(1809–1882)

Title

*The zoology of the voyage
of H.M.S. Beagle, under the
command of Captain Fitzroy,
R.N., during the years of
1832 to 1836*

Imprint

London: Smith, Elder,
and Co., 1839–1843

1. Seeking to collect a specimen of this rare Patagonian bird now known as *Rhea pennata*, Darwin's party shot and ate what they thought was an immature individual of another species. Upon closer inspection of the meal, Darwin realized they had eaten the bird he sought. The plate was illustrated by the great ornithological artist John Gould.

In terms of its lasting impact on scientific thinking, there has never been a more influential voyage of exploration than that of the H.M.S. *Beagle* from 1832 to 1836. Sailing out of Plymouth Sound Harbor in December of 1831, aboard the *Beagle*, on a voyage around the world, the young Charles Darwin embarked on an adventure in natural history that would ultimately ignite his determination to solve the "mystery" of the origin of species. Yet the voyage of the *Beagle* produced many more concrete discoveries in the form of thousands of specimens and accompanying notes carefully prepared by Darwin and his assistant. Ranging from fossil bones to crabs, and from rocks to beetles, birds, plants, and bats, Darwin's collections were shipped back to Cambridge to his friend and mentor, Professor John Stevens Henslow. Encouraged by Henslow's enthusiasm for his findings, Darwin returned from his trip in October 1836, determined to publish his geological observations and to find able naturalists to identify and describe the geological, paleontological, and biological wealth represented by his specimens. One of the outcomes of this effort was Darwin's *The zoology of the voyage of H.M.S. Beagle*, which appeared in five parts between February 1839 and October 1843. Darwin solicited donations from both public and private sources in order to publish this work, receiving support from the Duke of Somerset and the Earl of Derby, as well as a grant of £1000 from the Lords Commissioners of the Treasury.

The five parts of *The zoology* were each authored by an expert in the field, with different volumes variously including introductions and numerous notes by Darwin. Issued in numbered sections as they were completed, the parts included *Fossil mammals* (authored by Richard Owen), *Mammalia* (George Waterhouse), *Birds* (John Gould), *Fish* (Leonard Jenyns), and *Reptiles* (Thomas Bell). The final tome included 632 published pages and 166 plates. At the time of publication, the entire work could be purchased for £8.15s unbound, or £9.2s for a bound edition.

Each of the authors of the parts of *The zoology* brought his own style and background to the text, and Darwin's additions provided extra flavor. In the volume on *Mammalia*, George Waterhouse (then curator of the Zoological Society of London) provided technical descriptions of the included animals, while Darwin provided "A Notice of Their Habits and Ranges." The intimate nature of these notes lends a wonderful flavor to the otherwise technical prose of *The zoology*. For example, in the account for the bat *Desmodus*, we not only find a description and measurements of this animal, but also learn that:

2.

The Vampire bat is often the cause of much trouble, by biting horses on their withers. The injury is not so much owing to the loss of blood, as to the inflammation which the pressure of the saddle afterward produces. The whole circumstance has lately been doubted in England; I was therefore fortunate in being present when one was actually caught on a horse's back. We were bivouacking late one evening near Coquimbo, in Chile, when my servant, noticing that one of the horses was very restive, went to see what was the matter, and fancying he could distinguish something, suddenly put his hand on the beast's withers, and secured the Vampire. In the morning, the spot where the bite had been inflicted was easily distinguished from being slightly swollen and bloody. The third day afterwards we rode the horse, without any ill effects.

The illustrations accompanying the text of *The zoology* consist of a series of unsigned colored and uncolored lithographs depicting the animals described. The bat plates each include a full-body illustration of the animal and one or more portraits of the face. The latter are important because many bats have distinctive facial features including noseleaves—which are thought to help direct echolocation calls—and ears with characteristic size, shape, and projections. The combination of detailed descriptions and illustrations makes it possible for scientists today to unambiguously identify most of the species described in *The zoology of the voyage of H.M.S. Beagle*, despite the fact that many more species—many of them cryptic—are now known from the regions that Darwin visited. In the greater context of Darwin's life, many topics he later explored in his writings, especially his development of the theory of natural selection, harken back to his formative experience aboard H.M.S. Beagle and are documented in the *The zoology*.

2. The skull of *Toxodon*, an extinct Patagonian fossil mammal the size of a rhinoceros. Darwin's speculations on the extinction of such large mammals, and their apparent replacement by the small mammals now living in Patagonia, played a prominent role in his earliest evolutionary thinking.

3. The large Falklands wolf, *Dusicyon australis*, then known as *Canis antarcticus*, was remarkable for its lack of a fear of humans. Darwin suspected this quality would be its undoing and that it will "be classed with the Dodo." Hunted for its fur and because it was thought to be a threat to livestock, it was extinct by 1876.

4. A common vampire bat, now known as *Desmodus rotundus*. Blood-feeding bats were not well understood at this time, and George Robert Waterhouse, author of the *Mammalia* volume, thought it "remarkable" that this species lacked the type of teeth that would allow it to chew solid food, instead having blade-like teeth. As in most nineteenth-century depictions of bats, this vampire is shown in an unnatural pose. In nature, vampire bats use their large thumbs to aid in four-legged walking and scrambling to approach their prey.

Nancy B. Simmons is a curator in the Mammalogy Department in the Division of Vertebrate Zoology at the American Museum of Natural History.

Canis antarcticus.

3.

Desmodus D'Orbignyi.

4.

Equus Zebra Linn.

Schreber's World of Mammals

MIRIAM T. GROSS

Author

Johann Christian Daniel von
Schreber (1739–1810)

Title

*Die Säugthiere in
Abbildungen nach der Natur,
mit Beschreibungen*

*(Mammals illustrated from
nature, with descriptions)*

Imprint

Erlangen: Expedition
des Schreber'schen
Säugthiere und
des Esper'schen
Schmetterlingswerkes,
1774–1846

1. French artist Jacques
DeSève (active 1742–1788)
drew this fine portrait of
a Mountain Zebra (*Equus
zebra)* for the first edition of
Count Buffon's (1707–1788)
Histoire naturelle, générale
(1749–1804). Many of
DeSève's animal portraits for
that forty-four-volume landmark
encyclopedia were reused in
Säugthiere, as well as in other
publications.

Johann Christian Daniel von Schreber, born in 1739, was trained in medicine, natural history, and theology in his native Germany, and in Uppsala, Sweden. There, he studied botany with the great taxonomist Carl Linnaeus, a relationship maintained through correspondence for many years. Schreber edited and published later editions of several of Linnaeus's works, in addition to his own writings. Botany, especially the grasses, was his special subject, and several plants were named in his honor. A practicing physician, he was professor of medicine in Germany at the Mecklenburg and Erlangen universities. In Erlangen, Schreber was also professor of natural history at the university, and director of the city's natural history museum and botanical gardens. He was a member of the Royal Swedish Academy of Sciences, and, in 1791, was knighted.

Die Säugthiere, Schreber's best-known work, is devoted to all the world's mammals then known. Publication extended over seventy-one years, with work continuing long after Schreber's death in 1810. Georg August Goldfuss and Andreas Johann Wagner completed and published the final volume, and subsequently produced a supplement. The text describes each animal's appearance and behavior, and includes all known scientific and common names dating back to Pliny's *Natural history*. Gesner, Aldrovandi, Buffon, Cuvier, Daubenton, Desmarest, and other earlier illustrious naturalists are cited. *Säugthiere* is also noteworthy in that Linnaean binomial nomenclature was widely employed for the first time. Common names appear in many languages, including Russian, English, Spanish, Norwegian—even local dialects when appropriate (Lapp and Tartar)—as well as French and Italian.

But, impressive as Schreber's texts are, *Säugthiere* is best known for its engraved illustrations. This varied, enormous group of animal portraits confronts the researcher with a confusing smorgasbord of artists, engravers, sources, beautifully drawn accurate depictions (deer, elk, sheep, squirrels), and fanciful and often outrageously anthropomorphic portraits (primates). As has been true throughout the history of zoological illustration, the accuracy of illustrations varies according to whether the art was based on actual observation—whether of a specimen or a live animal—or was copied from an earlier depiction by someone who also had never seen that animal. The *Säugthiere* engravings include many examples of these extremes.

At least sixty artists are represented, including many of the finest animal illustrators of the late eighteenth century: Jean-Baptiste Audebert, Nicolas Maréchal, Jacques DeSève, Pierre Sonnerat, Johann Eberhardt Ihle, and Nicolas Huet are the best known. There are also numerous unsigned plates, and many with joint credits ("Ihle nach Audebert" and "Nach Maréchal gez. von Ihle"), and, mysteriously, in the American Museum of Natural History's copy, several watercolor drawings either adjacent to a matching print or inserted as a replacement. On the verso of each is penciled "Exact copy made by Friedlander, 1932."

Exemplifying Schreber's reuse of previously published illustrations are some of Audebert's monkey portraits, published originally in 1800, in his *Histoire naturelle des singes et des makis.* An intrepid and dedicated researcher could spend a great deal of time tracing the provenance of the *Säugthiere* art, and, indeed, this has been attempted: C. Davies Sherborn's exhaustive study "On the Dates of the Parts, Plates, and Text of Schreber's 'Säugthiere'" was published in 1891, in *The Proceedings of the Zoological Society of London.*

My involvement with the *Säugthiere* engravings began in an unusual way. In 1989, as I was organizing the exhibition "Kingdoms of Land, Sea and Sky" for the New York Public Library, two colleagues showed me a group of 195 watercolor drawings "rediscovered" in the Rare Book Room stacks. The drawings, depicting a wide assortment of mammals, were in a "plain brown folder" labeled "Schreber's drawings (to his work on Mammalia)." The package had been sent from a Boston publisher to Dr. J. G. Cogswell/Astor Library, New York. Joseph Green Cogswell served from 1848 as the first superintendent of the Astor Library—one of the forerunners of the New York Public Library. Thus, the arrival of the art can be dated between 1848 and 1877, the year Cogswell died. Otherwise, its provenance is unknown.

Highly impressed with the quality of the drawings, I selected eleven for inclusion in the "Kingdoms" displays, two of which were also published in the companion book, *The animal illustrated.* Because the New York Public Library does not own Schreber's *Säugthiere,* I consulted the American Museum of Natural History's library copy, firstly to verify that these drawings were indeed the original art for the published engravings, and secondly for background information for exhibition label texts and book illustration captions. My fascination with *Säugthiere* continued after my retirement. Working alternately at both libraries, I was eventually able to match 163 of the drawings with the corresponding engravings, despite variations such as reversed images—not unusual in the transfer of a drawing into a print—and differing backgrounds and colors. I also wanted to learn more about the artists and engravers, and, mostly, more about the creator of this intriguing and beautiful encyclopedia.

2. This realistic depiction of a crested porcupine (*Hystrix cristata*), native to Africa and Italy, was drawn from life. The engraver, Johann Nussbiegel, deserves some of the credit for the excellence of this and many other fine *Säugthiere* illustrations.

3. A painted-from-life portrait of a spotted hyena *(Crocuta crocuta)* is quite realistic. The artist, Johann Eberhardt Ihle, provided many of the most accurate and visually outstanding illustrations for *Säugthiere.*

4. Only the flamboyant facial and rump coloration of the male mandrill (*Mandrillus sphinx*) establishes its identity. The majority of the numerous primate portraits in *Säugthiere* similarly deviate from reality, since the artists usually worked from specimens or copied earlier engravings.

5. This strange mammal with the baleful expression is identified as a meerkat, and is a prime example of many equally fanciful *Säugthiere* portraits. Meerkats (*Suricata suricatta*) are small, slender African carnivores. DeSève's portrait first appeared in Buffon's *Histoire naturelle, générale.*

Miriam T. Gross *is a volunteer in the Ornithology Department in the Division of Vertebrate Zoology at the American Museum of Natural History. She retired as Senior Librarian and natural history specialist in the General Research Division at the New York Public Library.*

Hystrix criftata Linn.

2.

Hyaena Crocuta.

3.

Simia Mormon Alftroem.

4.

Viverra Suricatta Buff.

5.

Sailing to the South Pole: Dumont d'Urville and the Discovery of East Antarctica

ROSS D. E. MACPHEE

Author
Jules-Sébastien-César
Dumont d'Urville
(1790–1842)

Title
Voyage au pole sud et dans
l'Océanie sur les corvettes
l'Astrolabe et la Zélée, exécuté
par ordre du roi pendant les
années 1837–1838–1839–
1840

(Journey to the South Pole
and in Oceania on the
corvettes Astrolabe and Zélée,
executed by order of the king
during the years 1837–1838–
1839–1840)

Imprint
Paris: Gide, 1842–1854

1. As this plate clearly insinuates, d'Urville, hoping to penetrate the Weddell Sea and thus sail to the South Pole, almost managed to get his vessels trapped in the ice. Sailing to the pole is, of course, impossible because it is situated on land—a matter finally settled in the early twentieth century.

Jules-Sébastien-César Dumont d'Urville—known as the "French Captain Cook" to his countrymen—undertook an expedition to the Great South Sea on behalf of the French navy from 1837 to 1840. The expedition had several purposes; one was to sail, if possible, all the way to the South Pole, which some believed to be situated in open ocean. On his second attempt, in January 1840, he did not find a route to the pole, but he did discover an unknown coast, which he gallantly named Terre Adélie, or Adélie Land, after his wife. On January 21, stepping onto an island just off its icebound shore, his men claimed Adélie Land for France. In so doing, they became the first humans to stand on the eastern, or truly continental, part of Antarctica.

By this achievement, d'Urville had also won a small victory in the larger global competition between the two European superpowers of the day, Britain and France, as well as besting a recent upstart, the United States of America. D'Urville's expedition was thus typical of the time: although the French government certainly wanted to keep an eye on British (and American) expansionism in the South Pacific, there was also much interest in discovering new sources of supply of seals and whales, charting coasts, cataloging compass deviation, looking for valuable minerals, and acquiring collections of hitherto unknown flora and fauna.

Having failed to attain the pole, d'Urville's squadron of two ships, *Astrolabe* and *Zélée*, left for additional explorations in the South Pacific, eventually returning to Toulon in November 1840, to great accolades. Tragically, d'Urville died only two years after his return to France, but in the meantime he had begun, with great industry, to edit as well as to contribute to the reports on the voyage's results (eventually comprising twenty-three volumes, published between 1842 and 1854). The scientific reports covered a wide swath, from anthropology to zoology. Before professionalization became the rule in science, it was usually ships' medical officers who did the collecting and describing, and the thousands of birds, mammals, insects, fishes, crustaceans, mollusks, and artifacts (and not a few human remains) carried home were mostly gathered by the squadron's three surgeons. When the chief draughtsman of the expedition fell ill and died, it was the surgeons who took on the job of drawing specimens and making notes on their physical features. These notes were invaluable when the collections were described for publication, often years later, and sometimes by other hands.

In the early nineteenth century, the engraved plate was still the cutting-edge for the presentation of pictorial information. Here we present a scenic view (figure 1) that was designed to illustrate the narrative of the voyage, and several natural history plates (figures 2–5) of the kind typically used to communicate scientific results. The

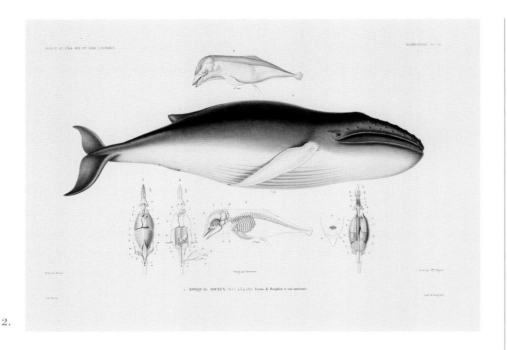

scenic plate presents a deceptively tranquil scene; in fact, at this time (February 6, 1838), both of d'Urville's ships were incarcerated in the ice, in danger of becoming beset. In the foreground, men hack away at the ice, to gather blocks to melt for fresh water. The strangely angled contraption in the background off the starboard quarterdeck may be a solar compass, and in the distance, men can be seen slaughtering seals. The bearded, bespectacled man in the foreground, brandishing an officer's sword in one hand and the severed head of a large seal in the other, is shown in such detail that he doubtless represents a particular person. Perhaps he was one of the colleagues of surgeon Louis Lebreton, whose drawing was used for this plate.

The humpback whale, evidently female, in figure 2, was probably sketched at the Chilean whaling port of Talcahuano, where d'Urville's officers were invited to watch a flensing operation—the process of removing the blubber from a whale. The plate is not especially accurate. For example, the whale's lower jaw lacks the row of "stovebolt" tubercles (nodules) that always line both jaw margins in humpbacks. Also, the pectoral flippers lack rugosities and barnacle encrustations, which are inevitably present on these animals. Humpbacks keep their jaws shut except when feeding; the partially open mouth seen here implies (unsurprisingly) that the animal was dead when drawn. The inclusion of several studies of a fetus is interesting, although there is no reference to it in the published text.

The existence of humpbacks in the southern ocean was already well known by this time, so perhaps the purpose of this plate was more about advertising commercial opportunities than science. Due to the catastrophic overhunting of whales in northern waters, whalemen were looking for other venues, and one of the expedition's main objectives was to identify new whaling grounds. This put tremendous pressure on whale populations everywhere, but especially on slow-moving, easily hunted species that could be caught and processed with the technology then available.

2. "Humpback Whale (*Megaptera novaeangliae*)." Voyages of exploration almost always had a commercial side, and the French and British alike were interested in developing sealing and whaling in the southern ocean. By the 1840s, slow, easily hunted species like right whales had become rare, and whalers were turning to other prey such as humpbacks.

3. "Warrior of Nuku Hika, Marquesas Islands." D'Urville's ships visited the Marquesas in late August of 1838 in order to collect artifacts and make ethnographical notes. Lebreton executed this exceptional drawing of a tattooed Marquesan warrior, or *toa*, wearing a traditional loincloth and idly handling a war club, or *'u'u*.

4. & 5. "Crabeater Seal (*Lobodon carcinophagus*)." Despite its name, the crabeater's distinctive teeth, seen here, are used to capture krill, not crabs. D'Urville's naturalists knew they had found an interesting new seal, but because of publication delays, the Englishman J. E. Gray managed to describe the species first.

Ross D. E. MacPhee *is a curator in the Mammalogy Department in the Division of Vertebrate Zoology at the American Museum of Natural History.*

3.

NATUREL DE NOUKA-HIVA.

4.

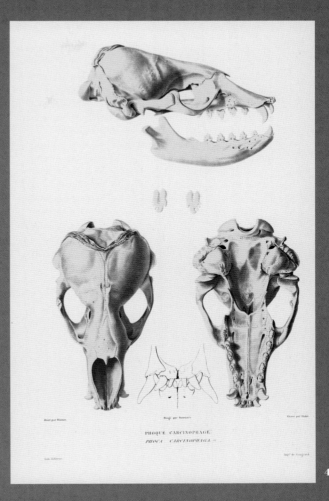

PHOQUE CARCINOPHAGE.
PHOCA CARCINOPHAGA.

5.

PHOQUE CARCINOPHAGE.
PHOCA CARCINOPHAGA.

PLATE XCVIII

Drawn on Stone by J.W.Audubon.

Lith.ᵈ Printed & Col.ᵈ by J.T Bowen, Philadᵃ

BASSARIS ASTUTA, LICHT.

RING-TAILED BASSARIS.

Natural Size.

MALE.

The Last Hurrah:
Audubon and Bachman's Mammals

MARY LECROY

Author
John James Audubon
(1785–1851) and
John Bachman
(1790–1874)

Title
*The viviparous quadrupeds
of North America*

Imprint
New York: J. J. Audubon,
1845–1854

A chance meeting in 1831 between John James Audubon and Reverand John Bachman on the streets of Charleston, South Carolina, set the stage for a collaboration between these two naturalists that would not bear fruit until more than fifteen years later. When they met, Audubon had returned from London hoping to secure additional subscribers for *Birds of America*, the printing of which was progressing. Their meeting reignited Bachman's interest in natural history and provided Audubon with a soul mate in its study.

As a child, Bachman had closely observed the natural world, and, later, as a student and teacher in Philadelphia, he concentrated on mammals. His careful and detailed studies led to his recognition as a serious scientist. After his meeting with Audubon, Bachman's spare time was devoted to mammal studies. In 1836 and 1837, he produced monographs on rabbits, mice, shrews, and, squirrels of North America.

Audubon and Bachman corresponded regularly, and, in 1838, when *Birds of America* was nearing completion, Bachman wrote to Audubon, "What you will do next, I know not," and suggested that a book on quadrupeds would be "serviceable to science" and perhaps profitable. Over the next several years, Bachman expanded his reputation, visiting European museums and becoming acquainted with mammalogists there. Audubon began painting mammals and charging ahead with plans for their book.

The years of collaboration between Audubon and Bachman were fraught with problems. Audubon's two sons had married two of Bachman's daughters, both of whom died of tuberculosis within a few years of marriage. Bachman's wife was an invalid, his own health was poor, and increasing responsibilities within his church organization left him unable to devote as much time and effort to their joint project as he would have liked. Audubon himself was becoming aware of his own advancing age and declining health.

Both Audubon and Bachman wished to expand the scope of their book to include western mammals, and a trip to the West would allow Audubon to make field observations and provide Bachman with additional specimens to study. Audubon's family was secure, for the first time settled on their own property in upper Manhattan, and *Birds of America* and the text volumes that accompanied it were finally complete, so Audubon could turn his full attention to the mammal book. Thus, in 1843, he undertook a trip to the upper Missouri River with a small group of friends, traveling as far west as Fort Union. Audubon wrote a glowing journal of life in the West at that time, and returned with mammal skins prepared by taxidermist John Bell, plant sketches by Isaac Sprague, and a menagerie of living animals. Yet Bachman was sorely disappointed by the scarcity of field observations.

1. "Ring-tailed Bassaris." The ringtail (*Bassariscus astutus*), as it is now known, is a nocturnal omnivore related to the raccoon. It ranges through the southwestern United States and into Mexico.

2.

Soon after his return, Audubon's declining eyesight made painting difficult and eventually impossible. Increasingly, his sons Victor Gifford and John Woodhouse Audubon joined Bachman for the completion of the mammal book. Both sons had remarried and had the support of their own growing families, as well as that of their aging parents, to consider. Bachman, who wrote almost the entire text of the mammal work, found himself without access to literature needed to make the work scientifically accurate. He was continually frustrated when his pleas for information and literature from the sons went unanswered, and his own health, never robust, remained fragile. By the time the elder Audubon was unable to continue painting, he had completed seventy-six plates. John Woodhouse then painted seventy-four. Bachman's constant pressure on the sons resulted in the publication of the 150 plates of *The viviparous quadrupeds* and Volume 1 of the text in 1846. John James Audubon lived to see that much of the joint work completed.

The second volume of text was published in 1851, the year John James Audubon died. Because of Bachman's own eye problems, that volume was dictated to and edited by Maria Bachman (née Martin), his sister-in-law, whom he had married after the death of his wife. In 1852, Victor went to Charleston to help with Volume 3 of the text, which was published in 1854 with six additional plates in Royal Octavo size, not in the Imperial folio size of the original 150 plates. Later in the same year, 155 plates and text were issued together in Royal Octavo size as *Quadrupeds of North America*. Thus, it was after so many years of struggle that this joint publication by Audubon, a world-famous ornithologist, and Bachman, a highly respected mammalogist, was at last completed. It is a lasting tribute, not only to the authors, but also to the many people who finally brought it to fruition.

2. "Nine-banded Armadillo." Audubon and Bachman thought the armadillo (*Dasypus novemcinctus*) resembled "a small pig saddled with the shell of a turtle." An animal of the southern and southwestern United States, it is most often abroad at night, searching for its insect prey.

3. "Townsend's Ground Squirrel." Townsend's chipmunk (*Tamias townsendii*), called a ground squirrel by Audubon and Bachman, was first described by Bachman in 1839. It is a lively inhabitant of coastal Washington and Oregon.

4. "Common Flying Squirrel." Flying squirrels (*Glaucomys volans*) nest in holes in trees and can be seen at dusk gliding diagonally from the tops of trees to neighboring trees by expanding the loose flaps of skin along their sides and using their flattened tails as rudders. These gentle creatures are rarely seen, but are not uncommon.

5. "Large-tailed Skunk." Known today as the hooded skunk (*Mephitis macroura*), this species, like all skunks, protects itself by spraying an odoriferous secretion to deter predators. It forages at night for insect and small vertebrate prey.

Mary LeCroy is a research associate in the Ornithology Department in the Division of Vertebrate Zoology at the American Museum of Natural History.

3.

Drawn from Nature by J. J. Audubon, F.R.S. F.L.S.   Lith. Printed & Col.d by J. T. Bowen, Phila. 1845.

TAMIAS TOWNSENDII. BACHMAN.

TOWNSEND'S GROUND SQUIRREL.

Natural Size.

N.º 6.   PLATE XXVIII.

PTEROMYS VOLUCELLA, GMEL.

COMMON FLYING SQUIRREL.

Natural Size.

4.

N.º 21.   PLATE CII.

MEPHITIS MACROURA, LICHT.

LARGE TAILED SKUNK.

Natural Size.

5.

Transported to Another Planet:
John Gould's The Mammals of Australia

ROBIN BECK

Author
John Gould
(1804–1881)

Title
The mammals of Australia

Imprint
London: John Gould (Taylor and Francis), 1863

Born in Lyme Regis, Dorset, in 1804, John Gould first rose to prominence in British zoological circles as a skilled taxidermist, becoming the first "Curator and Preserver" of the museum of the newly established Zoological Society of London in 1827. His lifelong passion for birds was soon recognized, and by 1833 he was superintendent of the ornithological department of the society. It was Gould who recognized that the diverse "blackbirds, gross-bills and finches" collected by Charles Darwin in the Galapagos Islands were, in fact, all closely related species of ground finch, a finding that was instrumental in leading Darwin to first question whether species are immutable.

From 1830 onward, Gould became famous for his magnificent ornithological monographs, lavishly illustrated with hand-colored lithographic plates, most of which were drawn (based on his own preliminary sketches) by his wife, Elizabeth. Sold in numbers of only a few hundred to wealthy subscribers, these impressive works led to inevitable comparisons with those of his American contemporary John Audubon. In May 1838, with a mammoth five-volume monograph on the birds of Europe recently completed, Gould embarked on a four-month sea voyage to Australia, seeing a golden opportunity to produce the definitive work on its unique, but as yet poorly known, avian fauna.

Although Gould traveled to Australia expressly to study its bird life, he was soon equally fascinated by its mammals, later writing that "[i]t was not . . . until I arrived in the country, and found myself surrounded by objects as strange as if I had been transported to another planet, that I conceived the idea of devoting a portion of my attention to the mammalian class of its extraordinary fauna." After two years collecting and drawing the native fauna, Gould and Elizabeth (who had accompanied her husband to Australia) returned to England, leaving behind an assistant, John Gilbert, to continue adding to Gould's collection. On their arrival in August 1840, husband and wife immediately began preparing *The birds of Australia* for publication, but tragically Elizabeth died within a year, shortly after the birth of their eighth child. Undaunted, Gould quickly hired the young artist Henry Constantine Richter to draw the remaining plates. The seven volumes of *The birds of Australia* were completed in 1848, by which time Gould had already begun to publish what is today perhaps his most famous work, *The mammals of Australia*.

Published in Imperial folio (22 by 15 inches) in thirteen parts between 1845 and 1863 (with an introduction published as a separate work in 1863 that includes updates and corrections), *The mammals of Australia* is an extraordinary record both of the Australian mammalian fauna and of nineteenth-century naturalists' perceptions of it. It documents a remarkable period of discovery, with Europeans struggling

1. "The Thylacine (*Thylacinus cynocephalus*)." By the time of European colonization, this superficially dog-like, carnivorous marsupial was restricted to the island of Tasmania, but it had previously also occurred on the Australian mainland. The thylacine was heavily persecuted because of its supposed threat to the colonists' sheep, with the last known individual dying in captivity in 1936.

2.

2. "Gould's Mouse (*Pseudomys gouldii*)." One of Australia's many species of native mice and rats, Gould's mouse was last seen in 1857. However, it may in fact be the same species as the Shark Bay mouse (*Pseudomys fieldi*), which still survives on four small islands off the coast of Western Australia.

3. "The Honey Possum, or Noolbenger (*Tarsipes rostratus*)." Known only from Western Australia, this beautiful little marsupial feeds exclusively on pollen and nectar from various species of flowers, which it collects with a long, brush-like tongue.

4. "The Yellow-Footed Rock Wallaby (*Petrogale xanthopus*)." Rock wallabies live in small groups on rocky outcrops, hopping over the steep terrain with remarkable agility. One species, the brush-tailed rock wallaby (*Petrogale penicillata*), has established a feral population on the Hawaiian island of Oahu.

5. "The Platypus (*Ornithorhynchus anatinus*)." Gould received contradictory accounts from Australian aborigines as to whether this bizarre mammal lays eggs, and he concluded that it did not. Definitive proof that the platypus and its relative, the echidna, are indeed egg-laying was not obtained until 1884.

to come to grips with the distinctiveness and often sheer strangeness of Australia's mammals. Most memorable of all are the 182 lithographic plates—drawn by Richter based on drawings and watercolors by Gould and his late wife, and hand colored by a team of colorists led by Gabriel Bayfield—which accompany Gould's text. Although varying in scientific accuracy, each is executed with a charm and vivacity that has rarely been equaled.

Some of the plates have become famous in their own right, with that of a pair of thylacines ("Tasmanian tigers") particularly iconic. Today, a recognizable reproduction adorns the label of Cascade lager from Tasmania. Poignantly, *The mammals of Australia* would also be something of a requiem for many of the species included within its pages: in the hundred years or so following its publication, the thylacine was exterminated from its final Tasmanian stronghold because of the threat it was thought to pose to sheep, while cats and foxes brought by European settlers precipitated a wave of extinctions among smaller Australian mammals on the mainland. Among the victims was Gould's mouse *(Pseudomys gouldii)*, named in 1839 by George Waterhouse in honor of Gould and last recorded in 1857—before *The mammals of Australia* had even been completed. Many other species are today much reduced in numbers and restricted to small fractions of the ranges indicated in Gould's book.

As with Gould's other works, only a few hundred original copies of *The mammals of Australia* were ever produced, and its cost put it beyond the reach of all but the wealthiest; original subscribers included large institutions such as museums and universities, but also numerous members of the British nobility and Queen Victoria herself. Today, complete originals are worth hundreds of thousands of dollars, with the last few to be auctioned subsequently dismembered so that the plates could be sold individually. The American Museum of Natural History is fortunate to have an intact copy of this remarkable work.

Robin Beck *is a research associate and former post-doctoral researcher in the Mammalogy Department in the Division of Vertebrate Zoology at the American Museum of Natural History.*

3.

PETROGALE XANTHOPUS, *Grey*

4.

ORNITHORHYNCHUS ANATINUS.

Drawn and on stone by H.C. Richter, del. et lith.   *Hullmandel & Walton, Imp.*

5.

The Perfect Performance of a
Particular Kind of Work

ELEANOR STERLING

Author
Sir Richard Owen
(1804–1892)

Title
Monograph on the aye-aye

Imprint
London: Taylor and Francis,
1863

Victorian England hosted a wealth of colorful scientists who dedicated their lives to piecing together patterns to better understand how the world works. It was an exciting time for biologists with sufficient information to be able to synthesize an ever-growing set of observations on the morphology, behavior, and distribution of plants and animals, with the goal of refining categories and delimiting species and their relationships to one another. An increasing number of explorers were also on the hunt for odd organisms that defied categorization, or at least tested the boundaries of the developing categories. The exploits of and, particularly, arguments between passionate scientists aired not just in meetings and written proceedings, but also in the popular press. Sir Richard Owen was at the epicenter of many of the crucial debates of the time. He stirred controversy with his ambition to create a National Museum of Natural History, as well as with his views on evolution.

An accomplished naturalist—with a six-decade career, more than six hundred scientific papers published, and a stint as a biology tutor to Queen Victoria's children—Owen worked for most of his life either in or for museums. The collections in these museums allowed him to meticulously compare the anatomical features of different animals and to study both fossil and extant species.

Owen is probably best known today for having coined the term "dinosaur," but his work on primates was unsurpassed at its time. Owen was particularly taken with an unusual primate, the aye-aye (*Daubentonia madagascariensis*), which is found only on the island nation of Madagascar. For the first one hundred years after the first aye-aye was brought to Europe in the 1780s, debate swirled over whether it was a rodent (a squirrel or tarsier—the latter having been classified as a rodent at the time), a primate, or most closely related to a kangaroo. The root of this confusion lay in the aye-aye's odd collection of behavioral and morphological traits that make it appear to be comprised of spare parts of other animals: the aye-aye has continuously growing front teeth (a rodent-like character and not common in primates), bat-like ears, a fox-like tail, abdominal mammary glands, claws on most digits, and spindly, dexterous middle fingers. It uses its middle finger to tap along a branch and moves its ears forward and back to help locate hollow channels within the wood—created by wood-boring insect larvae. Once it detects a channel, it uses its specialized front teeth to pry open the wood and then inserts one of its fingers to extract the larvae.

Owen definitively put arguments about the aye-aye's taxonomy to rest in 1863, with his elegant and, at times, lyric *Chiromys madagascariensis Cuvier* (*Monograph on the aye-aye*), which opens with a description of the history of scientific study on the aye-aye and moves to a painstakingly detailed description of its anatomy. This description focuses attention away from the striking unusual characteristics, like

1. An adult male aye-aye moving along a branch.

141

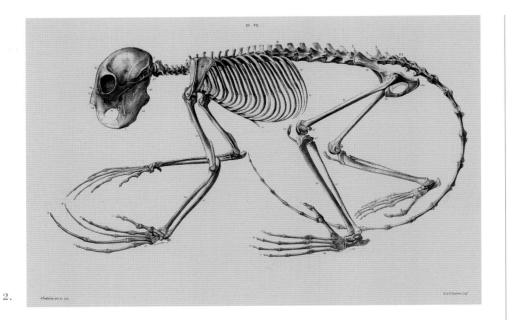

2.

2. An illustration of an aye-aye skeleton, showing shovel-shaped, continuously growing front teeth, long digits, and primate-like characters, including a large brain case in relation to the body size.

3. An adult male head, depicting large, hairless ears used in locating insect larvae, and forward-facing large eyes that help the aye-aye to navigate during the night.

4. An adult male aye-aye searching for insect larva within wood.

5. A young female aye-aye moving along a branch, showing clearly the filiform middle finger as well as primate-like opposable hallux.

the continuously growing teeth, and toward primate-like characteristics, such as forward-facing eyes and an opposable thumb, providing firm evidence for why the aye-aye should be classified as a primate.

Stunningly beautiful hand-colored lithographic illustrations of the pelage (coat), skeleton, and unusual morphological features accompany the text. The illustrator, Joseph Wolf, was one of the most accomplished of animal painters. He not only studied the alcohol specimen that Owen had received in 1859, but also watched the activities of a young female aye-aye in the London Zoo. The aye-aye is a nocturnal creature, which meant that Wolf had to observe the animal at night by candlelight. Mirroring Owen's emphasis on both anatomy and behavior, Wolf captures the mannerisms of the animals in his depictions of aye-ayes looking for insect larvae or traveling along a branch.

Owen paired his observations on the aye-aye's unusual anatomy with accounts of its behavior to narrate a story of a tight relationship between physical and behavioral traits—what he called "perfect adaptations of particular mechanical instruments to particular functions—of feet to grasp, of teeth to erode, of a digit to feel and to extract." He further notes a suite of interrelated modifications between morphological characters and the nervous system and sense organs—"of eyes to catch the least glimmer of light, of ears to detect the feeblest grating of sound, the whole determining a compound mechanism to the perfect performance of a particular kind of work." He stirred controversy via this monograph by using the synchrony of these adaptations to bolster his case against Lamarckian inheritance, as well as Darwinian evolution. While Owen participated critically in these debates, with this monograph a prime example, his primary focus continued to be on the establishment of the National Museum of Natural History, an endeavor he finally accomplished in 1881.

Eleanor Sterling is the Director of the Center for Biodiversity and Conservation at the American Museum of Natural History.

Pl. VI.

Pl. III.

3.

J. Wolf, del¹. J. Smit del., lith.

M. & N. Hanhart, Imp¹

J. Wolf, del¹. J. Smit del., lith.

M. & N. Hanhart, Imp¹

4.

Pl. II.

J. Wolf, del¹. J. Smit del., lith.

M. & N. Hanhart, Imp¹.

5.

DIPHYLLODES RESPUBLICA

Elliot's Jewels: Birds in Paradise

JOEL L. CRACRAFT

Author
Daniel Giraud Elliot
(1835–1915)

Title
*A monograph of the
Paradiseidae, or
birds of paradise*

Imprint
London: D. G. Elliot, 1873

1. This species, *Diphyllodes respublica*, is restricted to two small islands, Waigeo and Batanta, west of mainland New Guinea. Both sexes have blue bare skin on their crown. In the nineteenth century, artists had little information about mating behavior of birds of paradise, and the poses depicted are incorrect. Instead, the male displays on small vertical branches near the ground.

Daniel Giraud Elliot was one of the most important American ornithologists and naturalists of the nineteenth century. Despite his importance and stature, there is remarkably little recorded about his life's details other than what he wrote and spoke about his professional life in 1914, in an unpublished reminiscence and an address to the Linnean Society of New York. Nearly all testimonials and obituaries copied or paraphrased these two sources of information. Elliot's professional accomplishments were anything but obscure, however. He was a scientific founder of the American Museum of Natural History in 1869, and his personal collection of North American birds included the first specimens accessioned into the museum.

Elliot made numerous trips across the globe for study and collecting, generally being away for multiple years at a time, with his longest absence being a decade. Based on these travels, he published hundreds of papers, including multiple folio-size monographs on groups of mammals and birds, such as *A monograph of the Paradiseidae, or birds of paradise*, which was published in London in 1873. His scientific productivity was remarkable, given that his formal education was minimal—he withdrew from Columbia College shortly after his acceptance due to "delicate" health, but yet almost immediately set out for several years of travel in South America, Europe, and the Middle East.

According to those who knew him, Elliot was an imposing and courtly man. His soft-spoken, congenial personality no doubt facilitated his access to the world's museums and scientists—allowing him to spend months at a time in those institutions—but, importantly also, it gave him access to social circles of the wealthy and powerful, who became sponsors of his major works. Through his contacts in Europe, he assembled collections of birds for the American Museum of Natural History, most through purchases from dealers as well as from the personal collections of royalty and the wealthy. In today's parlance, Elliot was a networker.

Elliot must also have been a person of iron will and focus, with a drive to work long days and live through arduous travels to achieve his scientific goals. In his day, few, if any, of his peers had his knowledge and experience with the birds and mammals of the world. Elliot became famous as a monographer of families of birds and mammals. He synthesized previous taxonomic knowledge about the species in each group, and added observations and new interpretations based on specimens housed in major museums.

Elliot's first love was birds, and he produced large synthetic works on pittas, pheasants, grouse, hummingbirds, and birds of paradise. Along the way he also published a folio-size monograph on cats. In 1894, he moved to the Field Museum

2.

of Natural History in Chicago as its curator in the Department of Zoology, shifting his attention to mammals. After he left that museum in 1906, he spent the next two years traveling in Europe and Asia studying primates, both in collections and in the field. Next, back in New York at the American Museum of Natural History, his investigations eventually culminated in his 1913 three-volume taxonomic monograph *A review of the primates*.

During Elliot's time, folio-size, lavishly illustrated scientific monographs were primarily for the well-to-do and not meant for general distribution. They were funded by the wealthy and published for them. Elliot did not invent the monograph—indeed, in his youth, he was influenced by the works of John James Audubon—but he elevated its importance, combining the emerging field of wildlife art with contemporary science. Illustrative of that was *A monograph of the Paradiseidae*, published in London in 1873. It was "printed for the subscribers, by the author," and among those forty-nine patrons were many dukes, counts, earls, bankers, such as Baron A. de Rothschild, and a handful of institutional libraries. In 1887, Elliot's large ornithological library was purchased for the American Museum of Natural History by Cornelius Vanderbilt and Percy Pyne, and it was presumably at this time that this volume came to the museum.

A monograph of the Paradiseidae is a large folio with thirty-seven hand-colored lithographs. It is dedicated to none other than Alfred Russel Wallace, who along with Charles Darwin established an evolutionary world view within biology, and who wrote extensively about birds of paradise in the wild. The original water-color paintings for these superb plates were executed by Joseph Wolf (1820–1899), arguably the greatest wildlife artist of the nineteenth century. The lithography was undertaken by Joseph Smit (1836–1929), and the masterly colorist for the book was John Douglas White (1818–1897). Through a gift by Elliot's daughter Margaret in 1927, the American Museum of Natural History is indeed fortunate to have the original watercolors by Wolf, along with many of his wash drawings of these magnificent birds.

2. The Raggiana bird of paradise is well known for its long, flowing, red flank feathers. The wash drawing of Joseph Wolf, on the left, includes a small color guide for colorist John Douglas White. Close comparison with the published plate, right, reveals differences in details implying that this drawing was not the one sent to the lithographer.

3. Alfred Russell Wallace discovered this new species (later named *Semioptera wallacii*) in the Northern Mollucas (now Indonesia) in 1858—the same year that he wrote his revolutionary paper on natural selection.

4. The King bird of paradise is widely distributed in New Guinea. This species displays on horizontal branches, waving its highly modified tail feathers, and also by hanging upside down.

5. This spectacular form was named *Epimachus ellioti*, in honor of Elliot. Once thought to be a new species, scientists realized it was a probably a hybrid between the black sicklebill and the Arfak astrapia.

6. The twelve-wired bird of paradise is named for the long wire-like feathers above the tail used in courtship displays. The bright yellow flank feathers are due to pigments that fade to white soon after death.

Joel L. Cracraft *is the Lamont Curator of Birds in the Ornithology Department in the Division of Vertebrate Zoology at the American Museum of Natural History.*

SEMIOPTERA WALLACII

3.

CICINNURUS REGIUS

4.

EPIMACHUS ELLIOTI

5.

SELEUCIDES ALBA

6.

Books for the Naturalist in Everyone

BARBARA RHODES

> *Perhaps no study is more fascinating than the study of Natural History. . . .*
> *What lofty emotions can a single insect excite in our breast. . . . The flower of*
> *the field, the bird of the air, the fish of the sea, the creeping thing that creepeth*
> *on the face of the earth, are no respecter of persons. All may study their habits,*
> *examine their peculiarities, and admire their beauty.*
>
> The Naturalist (1856)

The blossoming of the gilt-stamped Victorian natural history book was made possible by a confluence of developments in book publishing, increases in literacy and leisure time, and the widespread enthusiasm of the age for the rustic and the natural. Adorned with gold foil, textured bookcloths, and embossed nature-related motifs and designs on their covers and spines, these books brought natural history to the Victorian masses, and in doing so, created a bookbinding art within itself.

The work of the naturalists of this era served to popularize science to the reading public, and soon networks of fellow enthusiasts formed, which led to the establishment of clubs and societies devoted to the study of natural history. One of the features of Victorian naturalism was the close and careful observation of the details of natural objects, sometimes with one of the newly available inexpensive microscopes, followed by the making of catalogs and lists of these objects and, often, the publication of these observations. Anything in nature could be observed and collected: insects and other invertebrates, shells, eggs, rocks, and plants—such as ferns—were among the most popular objects of study.

The study of natural history was also equated with adventure, as intrepid scientific explorers wrote about their travels to far-off lands. Books about these adventures, which were extremely popular, often featured scenes of exotic animals and people on their colorful covers, to attract the eye of the potential reader. If most Victorians could not manage an exotic expedition, their reach had at least been considerably expanded by new means of transportation, such as railways. Taking trains to the seashore and into the countryside meant sitting for long stretches with nothing to do, and what better way to improve one's traveling time than to read a lively and entertaining book about the wonders one was about to encounter?

Cloth bindings for books had been introduced in England in the 1820s, and by the middle of the 1830s, the covers had begun to be produced separately from the books themselves. This innovation made it possible to bind books much more cheaply and quickly, which in turn led to larger editions, as more people could afford to buy them. But how could they make them attractive to a public that was used to more substantial leather bindings?

1. The cover of John G. Wood's *Common moths of England*, published in 1870, exemplifies the tasteful use of gilt and black stamping on book covers of the period (later designs tended to be less restrained). The design combines popular images of Lepidoptera and ferns with a somewhat Asian appearance overall, reflecting another enthusiasm of the day.

2.

2. By the 1850s, gilt-stamped designs were intended to both attract the eye and to advertise the volume's content. They often graced the spines of clothbound books on natural history. In fact, on some books the spines actually received more decoration than the boards, as publishers realized that gilt stamping is what the potential buyer would see on the bookseller's shelf. The next-to-last book, at left, *Travels in the East Indian Archipelago*, features a detailed depiction of a palm tree and was written by the museum's founder, Albert Smith Bickmore.

3. This selection of gilt-stamped (and otherwise decorated) book covers, dating from 1847 through 1884, shows the wide range of subject matter that embellished the covers of natural history books in the latter half of the nineteenth century. The designs, which reflect the content of the books, from insects to birds and mammals, and from sea creatures to the sky above, were meant to attract a growing audience of natural history enthusiasts. Together, with the colorful book cloths embossed with a variety of textures, they gave the volumes a wide appeal at a reasonable price.

The first clothbound books had no decoration other than a paper label and the texture of the cloth itself, which was usually a smooth, polished cotton. However, the machinery to create embossed or printed patterns on cloth already existed, and had been in use by textile finishers for many decades. It was not long before bookbinders were making use of a wide variety of starched and embossed book cloths, some of the earliest of which were meant to look like leather.

Once the bindings were made, it was possible to decorate them by stamping them with heated brass dies, which became common by the mid-1830s. The cover boards were often stamped with a pattern which formed a frame; this was usually done "in blind," i.e., without using gold. Within this frame, the binder would stamp lettering or an image, called a "vignette," in gold foil. The spines of the books were also stamped in gold with the work's title and often another image.

At first, these vignettes were decorative images such as urns, lyres, and fountains, but by the 1840s and 1850s, the vignette had come to be more representative of the content; in fact, a sort of advertisement for the book. In many cases the cover decoration was a copy of one of the work's illustrations. Altogether, they form a rich and attractive heritage of natural history artwork.

Opposite, from left to right per row:
The ocean world, Louis Figuier (1872); *Handbook to the birds of Australia*, John Gould (1865); *The ferns of Great Britain*, John Edward Sowerby (1855); *An illustrated description of the Russian empire*, Robert Sears (1855); *Book of the black bass*, James A. Henshall (1881); *Stray feathers* (1878); *Life in ponds and streams*, William S. Furneaux (1896); *The illustrated natural history*, John G. Wood (1855); *Popular scripture zoology*, Maria E. Catlow (1852); *Days of deer-stalking in the forest of Atholl*, William Scrope (1847); *Wild life in a southern county*, Richard Jefferies (1879); *Queer pets at Marcy's*, Olive Thorne Miller (1880); *A manual of the Mollusca*, Samuel P. Woodward (1880); *Life in a whaler*, Charles Nordhoff (ca. 1870); *The life and adventures of Robinson Crusoe*, Daniel Defoe (1864); *A naturalist's ramble to the Orcades*, Arthur W. Crichton (1866); *Polynesian mythology and ancient traditional history of the New Zealand race*, George Grey (1855); *The tribes on my frontier*, Edward Hamilton Aitken (1884); *A natural history of the nests and eggs of British birds*, Francis O. Morris (1853–56); *Popular British entomology*, Maria E. Catlow (1860); *The land of the white bear*, Frederick G. Innes-Lillingston (1876).

Barbara Rhodes is the Library Conservator in the Research Library at the American Museum of Natural History.

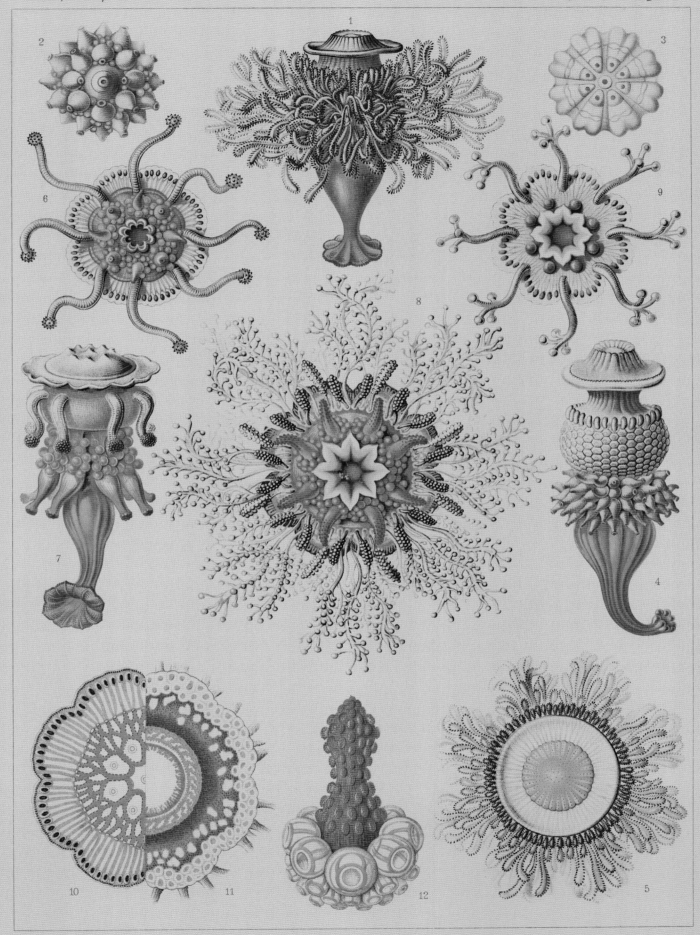

Siphonophorae. — Staatsquallen.

Seeing Is Believing

TOM BAIONE

Author
Ernst Haeckel
(1834–1919)

Title
Kunstformen der Natur

(Art forms of nature)

Imprint
Leipzig: Verlag des
Bibliographischen Instituts,
1899–1904

1. The Siphonophorae are an
unusual order of Hydrozoa. They
live in colonies whose members
are extremely specialized, but
also tightly integrated, so much
so that the colony often appears
to be a single organism. Many
of these siphonophorae colonies
resemble sea jellies and are
highly poisonous.

The well-traveled German biologist and popular professor Ernst Haeckel was scientifically and artistically active throughout his long career. A proponent of the then-recent and controversial theory of Darwinian evolution, he will be remembered by many for his inspirational and artistic renderings of the natural world's smallest and most geometrically symmetrical inhabitants. A keen observer of nature and a talented artist, this scientist's skills classifying and naming organisms under the microscope were well known even before he published the hundred groups seen in his *Kunstformen der Natur (Art forms of nature)*.

Haeckel honed his skill at the microscope as a scientist and illustrator of the enormous scientific bounty collected by one of the nineteenth century's greatest exploring expeditions—that of H.M.S. *Challenger* from 1873 to 1876. After the expedition, the collections were divvied up among the respective experts, and Haeckel was to examine the dredged up deep-sea finds. Included among the thirty-two volumes of published findings on zoology that were produced after the expedition were Haeckel's 1,804-page, two-folio text, and 140-plate atlas *Report on the radiolaria collected by H.M.S. Challenger*, which took him nearly a decade to complete. The work classified more than four thousand species of radiolaria (largely microscopic protists)—many described for the first time.

Haeckel had to edit his extensive portfolio of thousands of watercolor sketches to choose the subjects that make up *Kunstformen der Natur*. Through the work of lithographer Adolf Giltsch, his vision came to print. His hundred-image work was published in two forms—first in ten sets of ten illustrations in paper covers, produced between 1899 and 1904. Each set included an illustration and a printed description of the organisms depicted. To provide a key to the individual organisms—often crowded onto a single plate—a translucent sheet was laid over every plate, and each organism was outlined and numbered, the numbers referring to a key. This thin over-layer was tacked down at the edge, which allowed the viewer to clearly see the subjects below. The key on the following page described each of the many organisms seen. As Haeckel was especially enamored of radiolaria, each of the ten sets of ten plates, not surprisingly, includes at least one plate of this group.

The most striking element of Haeckel's illustrations in *Kunstformen der Natur* is the startling arrangement of the life forms depicted—especially the microscopic subjects. It appears almost as if some unseen magnetic force had aligned them and arranged each in perfect position for viewing. This maximized the real estate on the paper and allowed the greatest number of related organisms to be studied and admired. While the result was artistic, the intention was educational and scientific. For Haeckel, illustrating and sharing his observations was a way to convey

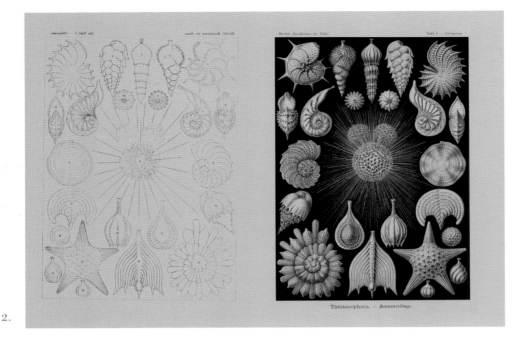

2.

2. "Thalmophora" is an older and unused term for foramanifera, or forams, the single-celled marine protozoa with shells. Their fossilized remains are invaluable for biostratigraphy studies, helping geologists determine the age of rocks based on fossilized remains of specific foram species.

3. Haeckel labeled these organisms "Aspidonia," a name no longer used. The grouping here includes members of the classes Merostomata and Trilobita. Most of these organisms are long extinct, except for those belonging to the class Merostomata, which includes the horseshoe crab.

4. The Ctenophorae (pronounced TEEN-a-for-ay) are often mistaken for sea jellies, but these transparent marine creatures are not closely related.

5. Asteridea is the subclass of echinoderms that includes the sea stars. While slow moving, they are high-level predators and feed on other invertebrates, including mollusks and barnacles.

6. The order Narcomedusae was named by Haeckel in 1879, and are distinguished by their bell shape with scalloped edges.

knowledge and information about the natural world. While some scientists observed and described connections between similar forms and functions to show relatedness between animals, Haeckel's vision and documentary skills went a step further, illustrating similar creatures together, so that anyone—scientist or not—could clearly see their relatedness. As a fervent believer in Darwinian evolutionary theory, he merely pointed out to his viewers the logic of the theory by providing them with a view by which they could see the obvious connections for themselves.

After five years, all ten sections of the work were complete, and owners could have the plates bound or the loose plates housed in portfolios. Due to the immense popularity of *Kunstformen der Natur*, in 1904, the entire set was published again in a second format, and all one hundred plates were available together. One of the American Museum of Natural History's two copies was received in a pair of handsome, paper-covered wooden boxes, with the work's title on the cover. Each of these "volumes" was designed to resemble a traditional book, albeit one with a hinged front cover. Inside, all the sets of plates and texts remain loose and unbound, presumably to facilitate ease in study, allowing viewers to spread the images out to make additional connections of their own without having to page back and forth in a bound volume.

From a solely aesthetic perspective, Haeckel's scientific illustrations, with their rich black backgrounds, fine-lined detail, and pleasant pastel palettes, are as appealing today as they were when first published. When one looks at artistic styles over the twentieth century, it's clear to see how Haeckel's work influenced movements from Art Nouveau to Surrealism, to artists active today. It is a testament to Haeckel's work that multiple editions reproducing his work remain popular and are still in print more than one hundred years after the publication of *Kunstformen der Natur*.

***Tom Baione** is the Harold Boeschenstein Director of Library Services in the Research Library at the American Museum of Natural History.*

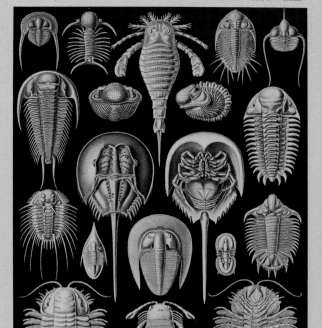

Aspidonia. — Schildtiere.

3.

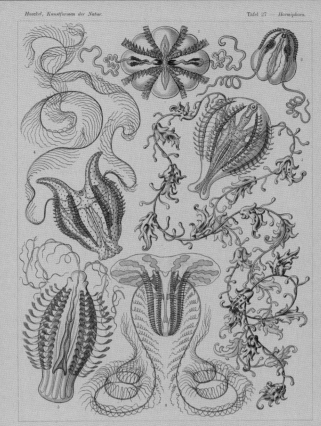

Ctenophorae. — Kammquallen.

4.

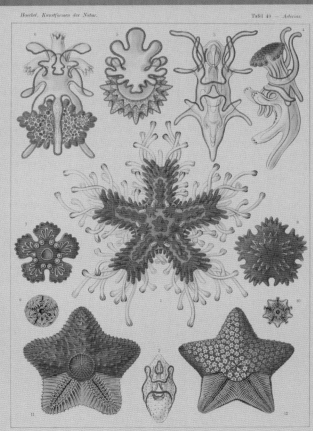

Asteridea. — Seesterne.

5.

Narcomedusae. — Spangenquallen.

6.

Fashion in the Natural World

STACY J. SCHIFF

Author
Emile-Alain Séguy
(1877–1951)

Title
Papillons: vingt planches en phototypie coloriées au patron donnant 81 papillons et 16 compositions decorative

(Butterflies: twenty phototyped plates in colored patterns, containing 81 butterflies and 16 decorative compositions)

Imprint
Paris: Duchartre et Van Buggenhoudt, [1925?]

Title
Insectes: vingt planches en phototypie coloriées au patron donnant quatre-vingts insectes et seize compositions décoratives

(Insects: twenty phototyped plates in colored patterns, containing 80 insects and 16 decorative compositions)

Imprint
Paris: Editions Duchartre et Van Buggenhoudt, [1929]

1. Plate 20 of *Insectes* is a composition of four inspiring design patterns in bright, contrasting colors.

Arguably the most celebrated of his eleven decorative albums inspired by natural forms, E. A. Séguy's *Papillons* and *Insectes* are a brilliant marriage of art, technique, and the natural world. Despite indisputable beauty, *Papillons*, commissioned by the American textile manufacturer F. Schumacher and Co. in 1920, and *Insectes* may be considered a curious acquisition for a natural history library. However, the insect specimens presented were chosen from scientific illustrations and re-created with the pochoir technique, giving them bold colors and details seldom seen by those outside the laboratory. Séguy showed the creative world how inspiring and captivating the colors, lines, and shapes of butterflies and other insects could be. And like members of the design and art communities, the scientific world took notice, too.

E. A. Séguy, a popular and influential French designer of patterns and textiles throughout the Art Deco and Art Noveau movements of the 1920s, is often confused with another E. Séguy (Eugene Séguy, 1890–1985), the well-known French entomologist with the same initials who published widely and who was a prolific scientific illustrator of dipteran insects (those with one pair of wings for flight and another for balance). Remarkably, many references to the artist refer to the scientist and vice versa. Background information on the pochoir artist, sometimes referred to as Émile-Allain, is scant, and the details of his life and origin are somewhat of a mystery. The entomologist Séguy certainly would have had no argument with the artist's observation of winged insects in *Insectes* as "mechanical wonders" of the natural world worthy of scientific study, as well as providing a muse for creating adornment for our interior world. Compositions of butterfly wings in *Papillons*, for example, speak to this philosophy, as they were intended to be used for wallpaper, textiles, and other elements of interior design and fashion.

For *Papillons* and *Insectes*, Séguy employed the pochoir technique, which is based on an ancient method in which stencils are used for color application. The stencils are cut out and applied sequentially to paper over outlines of artwork. Each color in the design has its own stencil through which layers of gouache, or other pigment, are separately applied by hand with a brush, or sponge, to provide a depth of color and texture. A costly and laborious process performed by highly skilled colorists, pochoir reached its zenith in Paris in the 1920s. Séguy's plates are exquisite examples of this practice that wonderfully highlights, as he wrote, "the intensity . . . shapes . . . and architecture . . . [of insects]." Séguy assures the reader in the introductions of his albums that the pochoir technique allowed for accurate color reproductions to give decorators true representations culled from scientific illustrations. Responding to a lack of resources for decorative artists on the magnificence and

157

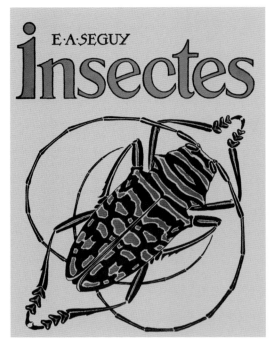

2.

detail of Diptera, Séguy writes in *Papillons* that he "sought to help [his] colleagues by carefully selecting the most beautiful specimens from the artistic point of view and reproducing them faithfully."

Previously unavailable in one place for study, Séguy offered exotic specimens in large scale for observation "without the tiring use of a magnifying glass." Although scientifically inspired, plates in these portfolios are presented for aesthetics, not for scientific arrangement. Wings overlap to maximize space on the page, and a group of butterflies rest together with wings open in spectacular color. In both albums, compositions follow the specimen plates to suggest the myriad of ways they may be utilized in decorative pattern, such as plate 20 in *Papillons* (figure 5) and plate 20 in *Insectes* (figure 1). The introduction serves as the only text, and each album has an index of specimen names with places of origin that correspond to the numbered specimens on each plate. The work is meant to be, as Séguy writes, "a miraculous wealth of harmonies and combinations of colors." Both portfolios display species from all parts of the globe, juxtaposing hue, shape, and variety. And while the specimens may never be found together in nature, they make for stunning designs of bold wings, bodies, and antennae that are in perfect synchronicity on the page.

The American Museum of Natural History Library acquired both its 1925 edition of *Papillons* and its 1929 edition of *Insectes* in 1930. Both publications consist of portfolios of loose plates contained between two folio boards with color illustration and cotton ribbon ties. Séguy also published similar portfolios showcasing prisms and flowers. Each plate is stamped by Séguy in the bottom-left corner of the page, complete with his trademark cluster of butterflies beneath his name in *Papillons*, and with a larger block of his name in *Insectes*. Séguy fused science with art, "fashion in the natural world," as he wrote in *Insectes*. Reproduced in countless forms on wallpapers, plates, and textiles for almost a century, Séguy's work continues to not only bring inspiration to many but also still garner enthusiasm from art lovers and scientists alike.

2. The pochoir-printed cover of *Insectes* still retains fragments of its original cotton ribbon ties.

3. Plate 5 of *Insectes* is a selection of winged insects in bold colors from tropical Asia, South America, and "Cosmopolite."

4. Plate 5 of *Papillons* is a selection of butterflies from the New World and African regions.

5. Plate 20 of *Papillons* shows a composition of arranged butterfly wings possibly intended for use in borders in the design of textiles and decorative art.

6. Plate 10 of *Insectes* shows a collection of five insects from four different continents, all with wings spread and illuminated in shades of copper and gold.

Stacy J. Schiff is the Visual Resources Librarian in the Library at the American Museum of Natural History. The author would like to thank Jonathan Elkoubi and Diana Shih for their translation work.

Pl. 5

3.

E.A. SEGUY.

Pl. 5

E.A. SEGUY.

4.

Pl. 20

E.A. SEGUY

5.

Pl. 10

E.A. SEGUY.

6.

ACKNOWLEDGMENTS

First, I'd like to offer praise to all the authors: it was a pleasure working with everyone, and I appreciate your allowing me to rope you in to this project. I must also thank all the prospective authors who had to listen to my unsuccessful pleas to get them involved in this project but declined nonetheless; thanks for listening.

All library staff deserve credit, including Louise Steward, who kept things running during this process, and especially Annette Springer, Susan Lynch, and Matthew Bolin, who were involved—whether they knew it or not—in respectively tracking down, borrowing, or purchasing reference materials for this volume. Gregory Raml and Barbara Mathe get my gratitude for patiently "giving me the finger" repeatedly upon request and without protest (the reader should think biometrically). Barbara Rhodes did what she does best, and the books praise her. I'm in debt to Mai Qaraman Reitmeyer, for her positive spirit and advice throughout this project; she has become a much-valued colleague in a very short time. Rachel Booth deserves thanks for all her good counsel, and Diana Shih, Dieter Fenkert-Fröeschel, and Mary Knight get extra thanks for all their patient translation work. Joel Sweimler and Vivian Trakinski's help as readers was valuable and much appreciated, and I must recognize Nina Root, my predecessor, for lending her two cents at many turns. Former librarian Mary DeJong, I hope, will be pleased to see that I've learned that these books contain far more than pretty pictures.

This project would not have been possible without Denis Finnin's expert photographic work. Aside from the historic photos in the foreword and introduction, Denis is responsible for every image in this book. It was a pleasure spending so many hours in the photography studio with Denis and with the stars of this project—the books.

Also, to the staff at Sterling Signature who ran this project (and me) with precision and sensitivity. I must acknowledge Editorial Director Pam Horn, Art Director Ashley Prine, Production Manager Erika Schwartz, and Editor John Foster for all their support and collegiality.

Finally, credit must go to Michael J. Novacek, the museum's Senior Vice President, Provost of Science, and Curator of Paleontology, for his encouragement and support throughout this project.

WORKS CONSULTED

Page 21
The Buyer's Guide to India, Circa 1678
Tavernier, J.-B. (1678). *The six voyages of John Baptiste Tavernier through Turky into Persia and the East Indies.* London: Printed for R[obert] L[ittlebury] and M[oses] P[itt].

Streeter, E. W. (1882). *The great diamonds of the world.* 2nd ed. London: George Bell & Sons.

Page 25
Made Merian
Davis, N. Z. (1995). *Women on the margins: Three seventeenth-century lives.* Cambridge, MA: Harvard University Press.

Page 33
Louis Renard and His Book of Extraordinary Creatures
Pietsch, T. W. (1984). Louis Renard's fanciful fishes. *Natural History, 93*(1), 58–67.

Pietsch, T. W. (1991). Samuel Fallours and his "Sirenne" from the province of Ambon. *Archives of Natural History, 18*(1), 1–25.

Pietsch, T. W. (Ed.) (1995). *Fishes, crayfishes, and crabs: Louis Renard's Natural history of the rarest curiosities of the seas of the Indies.* Baltimore: Johns Hopkins University Press.

Page 65
A Beautiful Harvest: Herbst's Crabs and Crayfish
Lai, J. C. Y., Ng, P. K. L. & Davie, P. J. F. (2010). A revision of the *Portunus pelagicus* (Linnaeus, 1758) species complex (Crustacea: Brachyura: Portunidae), with the recognition of four species. *Raffles Bulletin of Zoology, 58*(2), 199–237.

Page 69
At the Dawn of Malacology: The Salient and Silent Oeuvre of Giuseppe Saverio Poli
Burnay, L. P. (1985). Giuseppe Poli, fondateur des études de l'anatomie des mollusques bivalves. *Publicações Ocasionais da Sociedade Portuguesa de Malacologia, 4,* 9–12.

Castellani, C. (2008). Poli, Giuseppe Saverio. In *Complete Dictionary of Scientific Biography.* Retrieved October 8, 2011, from http://www.encyclopedia.com/doc/1G2-2830903466.html.

Catenacci, G. (1998). *Il tenente colonnello Giuseppe Saverio Poli, comandante della Reale Accademia Militare Nunziatella (1746–1825).* Molfetta: Associazione Nazionale ex Allievi della Nunziatella, Sezione di Puglia.

Ghisotti, F. (1993). La classificazione dei bivalve e l'opera di Giuseppe Saverio Poli. *Lavori della Società Italiana di Malacologia, 24,* 149–156.

Jatta, A. (1887). Giuseppe Saverio Poli. *Rassegna Pugliese di Scienze, Lettere ed Arti, 4,* 227–229.

Mastropasqua, L. (2007). *Lezioni di Storia Militare di Giuseppe Saverio Poli.* Napoli: Università degli Studi di Bari.

Morelli di Gregorio, N. (1826). Il cavaliere Giuseppe Saverio Poli. In *Bibliografia degli uomini illustri del Regno di Napoli.* Napoli: N. Gervasi (pp. [1–21]).

Tridente, M. (1950). Il molfettese Giuseppe Saverio Poli, antesignano della moderna biologia. *Archivio Storico Pugliese, 4,* 228–245.

Page 73
Pith Paper Butterfly Souvenirs
Crossman, C. L. (1991). *The decorative arts of the China trade.* Woodbridge, Suffolk: Antique Collectors' Club.

DeCesare, L. (2002). *Chinese botanical paintings, Tetrapanax papyferum (Hook.) Koch.* Retrieved June 6, 2011, from http://www.huh.harvard.edu/libraries/Tetrap_exhibit/chinesebotanicals.html

Williams, I. (2003). *Chinese drawings on pith paper.* Retrieved June 6, 2011 from http://www.chinese-porcelain-art.com/Chinese-Watercolours.htm

Page 77
Alexander Wilson and the Birth of American Ornithology
Allen, E. G. (1951). The history of American ornithology before Audubon. *Transactions of the American Philosophical Society, New Series, 41*(3), 387–591.

Christy, B. H. (1926). Alexander Lawson's bird engravings. *The Auk, 43,* 47–62.

Heston, A. M. (1904). *Absegami: Annals of Eyren Haven and Atlantic City, 1609 to 1904.* Camden, NJ: A. M. Heston, Sinnickson Chew & Sons.

Miller, L. (2010). *Alexander Wilson, father of American ornithology.* Santa Barbara, CA: John & Peggy Maximus Gallery; Santa Barbara Museum of Natural History.

Page 89
Discovering a New World: François Péron's Voyage to Australia
Péron, F. (2006). *Voyage of discovery to the southern lands: Books 1 to 3, comprising chapters 1 to 21.* (C. Cornell, Trans.). Adelaide: Friends of the State Library of South Australia. (Original work published 1807–1816).

Duyker, E. (2006). *François Péron: An impetuous life.* Carlton, Vic. Miegunyah Press.

Wantrup, J. (1987). *Australian rare books, 1788–1900.* Sydney: Horden House.

Page 93
From the Depths of the Sea: Risso's Pioneering Studies of Deep-Sea Life
Bourguignat, J. R. (1861). *Étude synonymique sur les mollusques des Alpes maritimes publiés par A. Risso en 1826.* Paris: J.-B. Baillière,1861.

Page 109
Burritt's Sky Atlases
Helfand, J. (2002). *Reinventing the wheel.* New York: Princeton Architectural Press.

Kanas, N. (2007). *Star maps: History, artistry, and cartography.* Berlin; New York: Springer.

Kidwell, P. A. (1985). Elijah Burritt and the "Geography of the heavens." *Sky & Telescope, 69*(1), 26–28.

Page 113
Alcide d'Orbigny: Darwin's Rival Naturalist
Berry, W. B. N. (1968). *Growth of a prehistoric time scale, based on organic evolution.* San Francisco: W. H. Freeman and Company.

Vénec-Peyré, M.-T. (2004). Beyond fontiers and time: The scientific and cultural heritage of Alcide d'Orbigny (1802–1857). *Marine Micropaleontology, 50,* 149–159.

Page 117
Colonel McKenney's Indian Gallery
Viola, H. J. (1976). *The Indian legacy of Charles Bird King.* Washington: Smithsonian Institution Press.

Page 145
Elliot's Jewels: Birds in Paradise
Allen, J. A. (1916). Daniel Giraud Elliot. *Science, 43,* 159–162.

Chapman, F. M. (1917). Daniel Giraud Elliot. *The Auk, 34,* 1–10.

Elliot, D. G. (1914). *Reminiscences of early days in the American Museum of Natural History.* (Unpublished typescript).

Jackson, C. E. (2011). The painting of hand-coloured zoological illustrations. *Archives of Natural History, 38,* 36–52.

Osborn. H. F. (1910). *History, plan and scope of the American Museum of Natural History.* New York: Irving Press.

Page 157
Fashion in the Natural World
Schleuning, S. (2008). *Moderne: Fashioning the French interior.* New York: Princeton Architectural Press.

INDEX